10 Minute Guide to WordPerfect®5.1

Katherine Murray

Doug Sabotin

SAMS

A Division of Prentice Hall Computer Publishing

11711 North College, Carmel, Indiana 46032 USA

To Mom and Pop—
(It's good to be the king.)
—ds/km

International Standard Book Number: 0-672-22808-4
Library of Congress Catalog Card Number: 90-

95 94 93   10

Interpretation of the printing code: the rightmost double-digit number is the year of the book's first printing; the rightmost single-digit number is the number of the book's printing. For example, a printing code of 92-1 shows that the first printing of the book occurred in 1992.

Acquisitions Editor: *Marie Butler-Knight*
Book Design: *Dan Armstrong, reVisions Plus, Inc.*
Manuscript Editors: *Pam Driggers, Ronda Henry, and Charles Hutchinson*
Cover Design: *Dan Armstrong*
Production: *reVisions Plus, Inc.*
Indexer: *Katherine Murry*
Technical Reviewer: *Joe Kraynak*

Printed in the United States of America.

Trademarks

Contents

Introduction

Perhaps you walked into work this morning and found that WordPerfect had been installed on your computer. There was a note stuck to your monitor: "We need a report to present at Friday's meeting. See what you can do." Now what?

A few things are certain:

- You need to learn the program quickly

- You need to identify and learn only the tasks necessary to accomplish this particular goal

- You need some clear-cut, simple-English help to learn about the basic features of the program

Welcome to the *10 Minute Guide to WordPerfect 5.1.*

Because most people are pressed for time and need to be able to get up to speed using new software programs quickly, the *10 Minute Guide* leads readers through the most important features of the program in a simple, "no-fluff" format.

And, because most users don't have the luxury of sitting down uninterrupted for hours at a time to learn a new program, the *10 Minute Guide* teaches readers the operations they need

1

in lessons that can be completed in 10 minutes or less. Not only does 10-minute format offer information in bite-sized, easy-to-follow modules (making operations easy to learn and remember), it allows users to stop and start as often as they like because each lesson is a self-contained series of steps related to a particular task.

What Are the *10 Minute Guides*?

The *10 Minute Guide* is a new approach to learning computer programs. Instead of trying to teach everything about a particular software product, the *10 Minute Guides* teach you only about the most often-used features in a particular program. Organized in lesson format, each *10 Minute Guide* contains between 20 and 30 short lessons.

You'll find only simple English used to explain the procedures in this book. With straightforward procedures, easy-to-follow steps, and special artwork (called *icons*), the *10 Minute Guides* make learning a new software program easy and fast.

The following icons help you find your way around in the *10 Minute Guide to WordPerfect 5.1*:

 Timesaver Tips offer shortcuts and hints for using the program effectively.

 Plain English icons appear when new terms are defined.

 Panic Button icons appear where new users often run into trouble.

Additionally, a table of features is included at the end of the book, providing you with a quick guide to WordPerfect features that are not given full coverage in this book. You can use this table either as a reference for more information or as a quick-guide to finding the keystrokes you need in order to perform routine operations.

Specific conventions are used to help you find your way around WordPerfect as easily as possible:

What you type	The information you type is printed in a second color
Menu names	The names of WordPerfect menus are displayed with the first letter capitalized
Menu selections	The options you select from the WordPerfect menus are displayed in bold type

Who Should Use the *10 Minute Guide to WordPerfect 5.1*?

The *10 Minute Guide to WordPerfect 5.1* is the answer for anyone who

- Needs to learn WordPerfect quickly

- Doesn't have a lot of time to spend learning a new program

- Feels overwhelmed by the complexity of the WordPerfect program

- Is a new computer user and is intimidated by learning new programs

- Wants to find out whether WordPerfect will meet his or her word processing needs

- Wants a clear, concise guide to the most important features of the WordPerfect program

Whether you are a manager, a member of an office support staff, a doctor, lawyer, teacher, business owner, or simply a computer novice, the *10 Minute Guide to WordPerfect 5.1* will help you find and learn the most important aspects of the WordPerfect program as quickly as possible. If your time is important to you and you need to make the most of it, you will find that the *10 Minute Guide to WordPerfect 5.1* helps you learn this extremely popular—and powerful—program in a fraction of the time you might ordinarily spend struggling with new software.

What Is in This Book?

The *10 Minute Guide to WordPerfect 5.1* is organized in a series of lessons, ranging from basic startup to a few more advanced features. Remember, however, that nothing in this book is difficult. Although most users will want to start at the beginning of the book and progress through the lessons sequentially, you can follow the lessons in any order.

If WordPerfect has not been installed on your computer, consult the inside cover for installation steps. If you need to review basic DOS commands used to prepare disks, see the *DOS Primer* in the back of this book.

This book concludes with a table of WordPerfect features that provides you with the quick keystrokes you can use to access the various features and lists references you can use to find out more about each item.

For Further Reference...

Look for these other Sams books that will add to your knowledge of WordPerfect:

- *The First Book of WordPerfect 5.1*, by Kate Barnes

- *The Best Book of WordPerfect 5.1*, by Vincent Alfieri, revised by Ralph Blodgett

- *WordPerfect 5.1: Step-by-Step*, by Judd Robbins

- *WordPerfect 5.1 Bible*, by Susan Baake-Kelly

Starting and Setting Up WordPerfect 5.1

In this lesson, you'll learn how to start and set up WordPerfect 5.1 for your computer system. You'll also get acquainted with the WordPerfect screen.

Starting WordPerfect

If you are using WordPerfect from floppy disks on a two-drive system, follow these steps:

1. Place the WordPerfect Program disk 1 in drive A and close the drive door.

2. Type A:WP and press Enter.

If you are using WordPerfect from a hard disk, follow these steps:

1. Change to the directory that stores the WordPerfect program files (for example, type CD\WP51 and press Enter).

2. Type WP and press Enter.

Startup Blues... If you need to review the basic DOS procedures for starting your computer, answering the date and time prompts, and changing directories, consult the *DOS Primer* in the back of this book.

The WordPerfect opening screen is displayed for a moment, and then the work area (known as the *edit screen*) is displayed (see Figure 1-1).

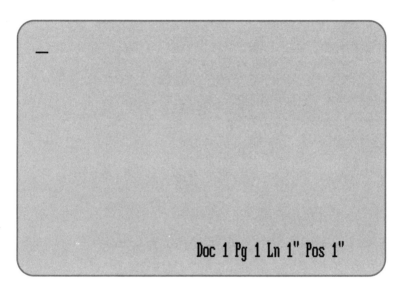

Doc 1 Pg 1 Ln 1" Pos 1"

Figure 1-1. The WordPerfect edit screen.

Setting Up the Mouse

If you plan to use a mouse with WordPerfect, follow these steps to set it up:

1. From the edit screen (shown in Figure 1-1), press Shift and F1 together. The Setup menu is displayed, as shown in Figure 1-2.

2. Type **1** to select the Mouse option.

3. Type **1** to select the Type option. When the Setup: Mouse Type menu is displayed, as shown in Figure 1-3, use the arrow keys to move the highlight to the type of mouse you are using. (If you are unsure, ask your dealer or check the manual that came with your mouse.)

4. Press Enter to choose the Select option.

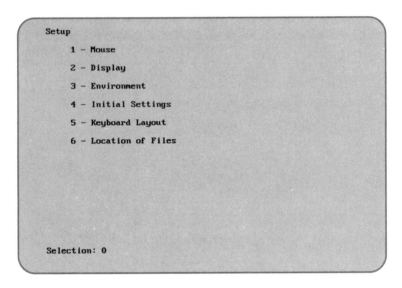

```
Setup

     1 - Mouse

     2 - Display

     3 - Environment

     4 - Initial Settings

     5 - Keyboard Layout

     6 - Location of Files




  Selection: 0
```

Figure 1-2. The Setup menu.

Setting Up the Menus

To a new user, the lack of helpful hints on the edit screen can be a little threatening. To display the menu options, follow these steps:

```
Setup: Mouse Type

    CH Products Roller Mouse (PS/2)
    CH Products Roller Mouse (Serial)
    IBM PS/2 Mouse
    Imsi Mouse, 2 button (Serial)
    Imsi Mouse, 3 button (Serial)
    Kensington Expert Mouse (PS/2)
    Kensington Expert Mouse (Serial)
    Keytronic Mouse (Bus)
    Keytronic Mouse (Serial)
    Logitech Mouse (Bus)
    Logitech Mouse (PS/2)
    Logitech Mouse (Serial)
    Microsoft Mouse (Bus)
    Microsoft Mouse (Serial)
 *  Mouse Driver (MOUSE.COM)
    Mouse Systems Mouse, 3 button (Serial)
    MSC Technology PC Mouse 2 (Serial)
    Numonics Mouse (Serial)
    PC-Trac Trackball (Serial)



1 Select; 2 Auto-select; 3 Other Disk; N Name Search: 1
```

Figure 1-3. The Mouse Type menu.

1. Press Shift and F1 together to display the Setup menu.

2. Press 2 to select Display.

3. Press 4 to select Menu Options.

4. Press 4 again and type Y. This option enables you to use the Alt key to access menus.

5. Press 7 and type Y. This option adds a line beneath the menu bar, keeping it separate from the edit screen.

6. Press 8 and type Y. This menu keeps the menu bar on the screen while you use WordPerfect.

7. Press F7(Exit) to save setup options and return to the document screen. The edit screen should now look like Figure 1-4.

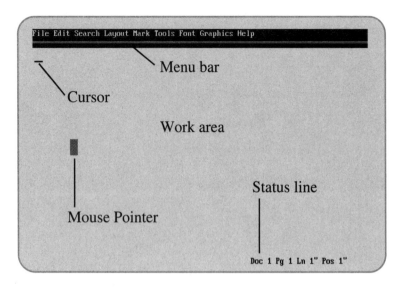

Figure 1-4. The edit screen with the menu bar.

The *menu bar* allows you to get to the pull-down menus easily. The *cursor* marks the place on the screen where characters will be inserted when you type. The *mouse pointer* shows the position of the mouse. The *work area* is the portion of the screen where you'll enter and edit text. The *status line*, at the bottom of the screen, gives you information about the cursor's location.

Quitting WordPerfect

Lesson 7 teaches you the basics of saving documents. If you want to quit WordPerfect without saving a document, follow these steps:

1. Press F7 (Exit), WordPerfect will ask you whether you want to save the document.

2. Type N for No.

3. When WordPerfect asks whether you want to exit the program, type Y for Yes. You are then returned to the DOS prompt.

Now you've started the program and modified WordPerfect so that you will be able to see and access the menus on the screen at all times. The next lesson shows you how to enter text and use the mouse and keyboard to move around in WordPerfect.

Lesson 2

Starting Your Document

In this lesson, you'll learn to enter text in your document, insert blank lines, and move the cursor using the keyboard and mouse.

Entering Text

Once the WordPerfect edit screen is displayed (refer to Figure 1-4), the program expects nothing more of you than simple typing.

Let's try it with the following paragraph. When you reach the end of a line, WordPerfect automatically moves text to the next line. This is called *wrapping*. Continue typing until you've entered the entire paragraph. (Don't worry about mistakes—you'll learn how to correct typing errors in Lesson 4.)

```
In the seminar Life Experience 101, leader
Leslie Sabotin takes you on a light-hearted
journey to a sometimes whimsical and some-
times intimidating place: your past. Explore
your experiences with words, music, sight,
and sound; spotlight your accomplishments and
perceived failures (by the end of this
seminar, the word "failure" will have been
forever stricken from your vocabulary).
```

At the end of the paragraph, press Enter. This inserts an invisible code called a *hard return*, which marks the end of the paragraph. Codes are explained in Lesson 6.

Inserting Blank Lines

To insert a blank line, simply press Enter when the cursor is at the start of a line. To see how this works with one example, follow these steps:

1. Press Enter.

This adds a blank line beneath the paragraph you just typed. The cursor should be resting on the line below the blank line.

2. Type the following line:

```
Credits: As many as you're willing to give
yourself.
```

3. Press Enter twice.

4. Now add the last line:

```
Prerequisites: An open mind.
```

Your screen should now look something like the one shown in Figure 2-1.

Moving the Cursor with the Mouse

Once you've entered text, you can use the mouse to move the cursor around. Follow these steps:

1. Move the mouse so that the mouse pointer in the work area is placed where you want the cursor to be.

2. Click the left mouse button.

13

Moving the Cursor with the Keyboard

You can also use the keyboard to move the cursor. Table 2-1 describes the keys you can use.

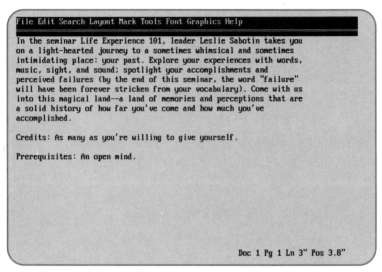

File Edit Search Layout Mark Tools Font Graphics Help

In the seminar Life Experience 101, leader Leslie Sabotin takes you
on a light-hearted journey to a sometimes whimsical and sometimes
intimidating place: your past. Explore your experiences with words,
music, sight, and sound; spotlight your accomplishments and
perceived failures (by the end of this seminar, the word "failure"
will have been forever stricken from your vocabulary). Come with us
into this magical land—a land of memories and perceptions that are
a solid history of how far you've come and how much you've
accomplished.

Credits: As many as you're willing to give yourself.

Prerequisites: An open mind.

Doc 1 Pg 1 Ln 3" Pos 3.8"

Figure 2-1. The screen after text has been entered.

Table 2-1 Cursor-Movement Keys

Key	Moves the Cursor
Up arrow	Up one line
Down arrow	Down one line
Left arrow	One character to the left
Ctrl-left arrow	One word to the left
Home-left arrow	To the beginning of the line or the left edge of the screen
Right arrow	One character to the right
Ctrl-right arrow	One word to the right
Home-right arrow	To the end of the line or the right edge of the screen

Table 2-1 (continued)

Key	Moves the Cursor
End	To the end of the line or the right edge of the screen
PgUp	To the top of the previous screen
PgDn	To the top of the next screen
Home, Home-up arrow	To the beginning of the document
Home, Home-down arrow	To the end of the document

Practice using a few of these keys to move the cursor through the document. When you start the cursor should be below the last line you entered.

1. Press up arrow five times. This takes the cursor to the second-to-last line of the large paragraph.

2. Press Home-right arrow. The cursor moves to the end—the far right—of the current line.

Now you've got the hang of entering basic text. In the next lesson, you'll learn to manipulate the menus in WordPerfect.

Lesson 3

Making Menu Selections

In this lesson, you'll learn to use the mouse and the keyboard to find your way around WordPerfect's menus and get help.

You can use WordPerfect with or without a mouse. Most users prefer to use a mouse for selecting menu options and use the keyboard for working with text.

Using the Mouse

If you haven't used a mouse before—or if your mouse experience has been limited—you may need to review a few operations you'll see used in this book. Using a mouse involves these procedures:

Point	Move the mouse pointer to an item on the screen
Click	Press and release the mouse button once quickly
Double-click	Press and release the mouse button twice quickly
Drag	Press the mouse button and hold it down while you move the mouse

Take a minute and try a couple of these procedures.

1. Move the mouse so that the mouse pointer is positioned on the word `File` in the WordPerfect menu bar.

2. Click the left mouse button once. The File menu is displayed on the screen.

3. Move the mouse so that the mouse pointer is positioned on the word `Edit` in the menu bar and click the left mouse button.

4. Move the mouse pointer off the displayed menu and click either mouse button. The menu closes.

Pull-down Menus The term *pull-down menu* refers to a menu that remains "hidden" in a menu bar until you use the mouse or press a key combination to open or "pull down" the menu. This type of menu gives you maximum space on-screen, yet still lets you get easily to the options you need.

Using the Keyboard

Even if you are using a mouse, you'll use the keyboard to enter text, edit text, and, in many instances, choose commands and interact with the program.

Try a couple of examples for keyboard practice:

1. Press Alt to use the menu bar.

2. Press the right-arrow key to move the highlight to the Edit menu; then press Enter.

3. Use the up- and down-arrow keys to move the highlight through the menu options.

4. Press F7 (Exit) to close the menu and return to the edit screen.

Using Speed Keys

Speed keys are function keys (F1, F2, etc.) that you use in combination with other keys to perform operations such as saving your documents or selecting menu items. The WordPerfect program comes with a keyboard template you can place over your function keys to help remind you which keys do what. A complete list of Speed keys is also provided on the inside back cover of this book.

Pressing Key Combinations When instructed to press two keys at the same time (called a *key combination*), press both simultaneously and release them immediately. Key combination instructions are written as Shift-F1.

Each function key actually performs several different functions, depending on which key you press with the function key. For example, pressing F1 cancels the most recent operation you've carried out, and pressing Shift-F1 displays the Setup menu, Ctrl-F1 displays the shell, and Alt-F1 starts the Thesaurus.

Each key combination is assigned to a different color on the template so you can easily tell which additional key (Ctrl, Shift, Alt, or none) you press for which procedure:

Ctrl	Red
Shift	Green
Alt	Blue
None	Black

Let's try using a function key combination. When only the menu bar and the status line are displayed on the screen, try this:

1. Press Shift-F1.

The Setup menu is displayed.

Take a few moments and experiment with the different function keys and key combinations. Remember that to get out of a procedure or to put away a menu, you press F7 (Exit).

Using the Menus

You use menus to work with your documents in a variety of ways. If you have not set the menu bar to display automatically (which we did in Lesson 1), you can display the menu bar one of two ways:

1. Press Alt.

   Or

2. Click the right mouse button.

Opening a Menu

Once the menu bar is displayed, select a menu in one of two ways:

1. Point to the menu you want and click the left mouse button.

   Or

2. Press the Alt key (if you haven't already done so) and press the highlighted letter in the menu name.

Selecting an Option

The next step involves making a selection from the menu. To choose an option,

1. Drag the mouse until the option you want is high-lighted, and then release the mouse button.

Or

2. Use the arrow keys to move the highlight to the option you want and then press Enter, or type the highlighted letter of the menu option.

If a particular option on the menu you displayed shows an arrowhead symbol in the right side of the menu, another pop-out menu will be displayed if you choose that option. Let's try it:

1. Open the Font menu.

2. Select the **Appearance** option.

Another menu is displayed, as shown in Figure 3-1. This contains the different settings you can choose for the **Appearance** option. To return to the Font menu, press Esc.

Getting Help

Even though you may be feeling comfortable with your new WordPerfect experience, there will be times when you get stuck and aren't quite sure what to do next.

You have a few options for getting help:

1. Place the mouse pointer on the Help menu name and click the left mouse button.

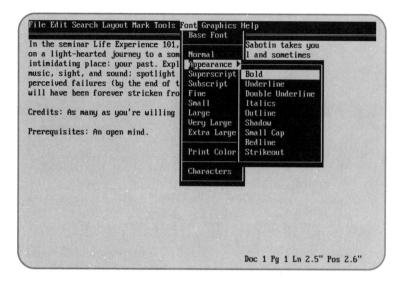

Figure 3-1. The pop-up Appearance menu from the Font menu.

Or

2. Press F3.

Or

3. Press Alt to move into the menu bar; then open the Help menu and choose **Help** (if you want to find out about using the help system) or **Index** (if you want to see a listing of help topics).

You can then choose the item you need by pressing the first letter of the option or operation or by pressing a function key to find out more about the procedures carried out by that key. For example, choosing **Template** from the Help menu displays the speed key template, as shown in Figure 3-2.

When you are ready to return to your WordPerfect document, you can press Enter or the space bar to exit the help system.

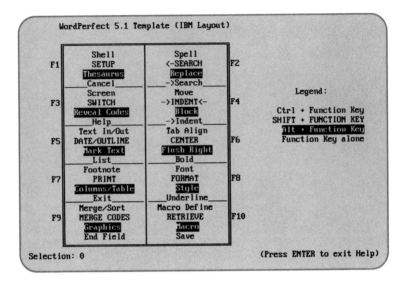

Figure 3-2. The function key template shown on the help screen.

In this lesson, you've learned to use the menus and get help. The next lesson shows you how to perform a few simple editing procedures.

Text Basics: Simple Editing Skills

In this lesson, you'll learn how to delete, undelete, and insert text.

Deleting Text

To correct simple typing errors—or make more sweeping changes involving words, lines, and even pages—you use the Backspace and Del keys. Backspace and Del work in slightly different ways:

- When you press Backspace, WordPerfect deletes the character to the left of the cursor.

- When you press Del, the program deletes the character at the cursor position.

Other keys, such as Ctrl, Home, and Esc, can be used with Backspace and Del to delete words or even entire lines.

Using Backspace To Delete Individual Characters

Using the document created in lesson 2,

1. Position the cursor at the end of the first paragraph.

23

2. Press Backspace two times.

WordPerfect deletes the character before the cursor—each time you press Backspace, the program "backs up over" another character.

Using Backspace To Delete Words and Characters

You can use Backspace to delete an entire word by pressing the Ctrl key with the Backspace key. Try it.

1. Position the cursor on the word *mind*.

2. Press Ctrl and Backspace at the same time.

WordPerfect removes the word *mind* as shown in Figure 4-1.

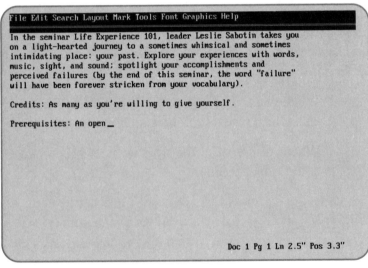

File Edit Search Layout Mark Tools Font Graphics Help

In the seminar Life Experience 101, leader Leslie Sabotin takes you on a light-hearted journey to a sometimes whimsical and sometimes intimidating place: your past. Explore your experiences with words, music, sight, and sound; spotlight your accomplishments and perceived failures (by the end of this seminar, the word "failure" will have been forever stricken from your vocabulary).

Credits: As many as you're willing to give yourself.

Prerequisites: An open _

Doc 1 Pg 1 Ln 2.5" Pos 3.3"

Figure 4-1. Deleting an entire word.

Using Del To Delete Individual Characters

The Del key works similarly to the Backspace key.

1. Move the cursor to the first letter of the word *forever*.

2. Press Del three times to remove the characters *for*.

Using Del To Delete Entire Words

To delete an entire word, you press the Home key along with the Del key.

1. Move the cursor after the remains of the word *forever*.

2. Press Home and Del together.

Each time you press Home-Del, WordPerfect deletes the word in front of the cursor, as shown in Figure 4-2.

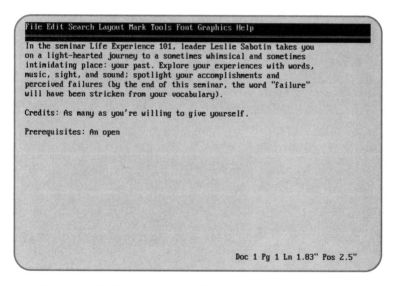

Figure 4-2. Text deleted with Del.

Undeleting Text

If you delete text accidentally, you may be able to recover it. WordPerfect "remembers" the last three sections of text you deleted. When you need to recover something you've just deleted, follow these steps:

1. Position the cursor at the point you want to insert the text.

2. Press Alt to move to the menu bar and open the Edit menu (see Figure 4-3).

3. Choose the Undelete option and type 1.

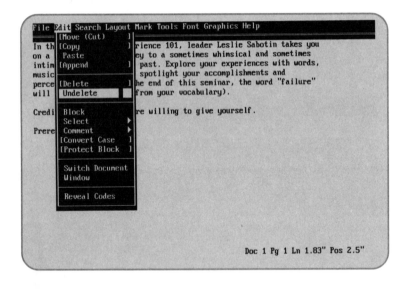

Figure 4-3. The Edit menu.

Inserting Text

WordPerfect makes it easy for you to insert text in your document. When you want to add text,

1. Position the cursor at the point you want to insert text.

2. Type the text you want to add.

WordPerfect adds the text you type and automatically realigns the paragraph when you use the arrow keys to move the cursor down through the document.

Insert mode When WordPerfect is in insert mode, the text you type is inserted at the cursor position. Any existing text is pushed to the right to accommodate the added characters.

Using Typeover Mode

Occasionally, when you type text, you want to replace text that is already there. For this reason, WordPerfect gives you the option of typing over existing text. To do this, you use typeover mode.

Typeover mode When WordPerfect is in typeover mode, any text you type overwrites (erases) any characters already there.

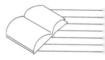

To put WordPerfect in typeover mode,

1. Position the cursor at the point you want to add text.

2. Press Ins. WordPerfect then displays the word Typeover in the status line at the bottom of the screen (see Figure 4-4).

3. Type the text.

The text you type then replaces the characters at the cursor position. To turn off typeover mode and return to insert mode, press the Ins key again.

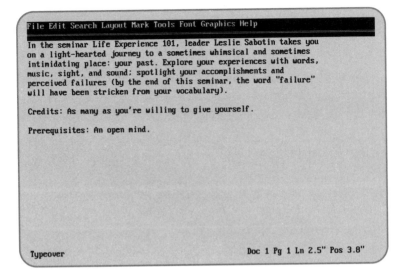

File Edit Search Layout Mark Tools Font Graphics Help

In the seminar Life Experience 101, leader Leslie Sabotin takes you
on a light-hearted journey to a sometimes whimsical and sometimes
intimidating place: your past. Explore your experiences with words,
music, sight, and sound; spotlight your accomplishments and
perceived failures (by the end of this seminar, the word "failure"
will have been stricken from your vocabulary).

Credits: As many as you're willing to give yourself.

Prerequisites: An open mind.

Typeover   Doc 1 Pg 1 Ln 2.5" Pos 3.8"

Figure 4-4. The document in typeover mode.

In this lesson you've learned to delete and undelete text.
The next lesson shows you how to enhance text by changing
text style and alignment.

Lesson 5

Text Basics: Enhancing Text

In this lesson, you'll learn to enhance your document by underlining and boldfacing text.

Underlining Text

WordPerfect enables you to enhance your text by changing the way the text looks. To turn on the underline feature, follow these steps:

1. Move the cursor to the place you want to begin typing in the new style.

2. Open the Font menu.

3. Select the **Appearance** option (see Figure 5-1).

4. Choose the **Underline** option from the pop-up box that is displayed and press Enter (see Figure 5-2).

5. Type the following text:

   ```
   We think you'll be pleasantly surprised!
   ```

6. Press the right-arrow key to turn off underlining.

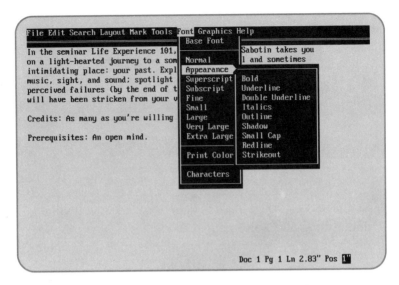

Figure 5-1. Selecting the **Appearance** option.

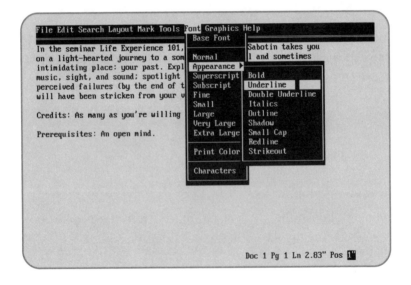

Figure 5-2. Choosing the **Underline** option.

The text you type is highlighted on the screen, showing you that WordPerfect has indeed placed the text in a new text style (see Figure 5-3).

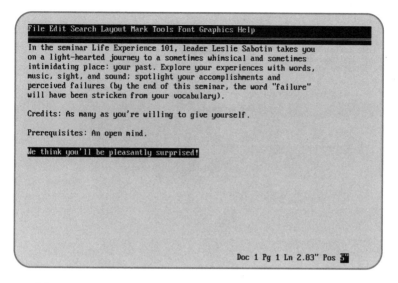

File Edit Search Layout Mark Tools Font Graphics Help

In the seminar Life Experience 101, leader Leslie Sabotin takes you on a light-hearted journey to a sometimes whimsical and sometimes intimidating place: your past. Explore your experiences with words, music, sight, and sound; spotlight your accomplishments and perceived failures (by the end of this seminar, the word "failure" will have been stricken from your vocabulary).

Credits: As many as you're willing to give yourself.

Prerequisites: An open mind.

We think you'll be pleasantly surprised!

Doc 1 Pg 1 Ln 2.83" Pos 5

Figure 5-3. The underlined text.

Boldfacing Text

The steps for adding bold text are similar to underlining:

1. Move the cursor to the place where you want to begin typing the new style.

2. Open the Font menu, select **Appearance**, and choose **Bold** (see Figure 5-4).

3. Type the following line:

   ```
   Special holiday rates.
   ```

4. Press the right-arrow key, and to turn off bold, press Enter.

WordPerfect adds the text in boldface type (see Figure 5-5).

31

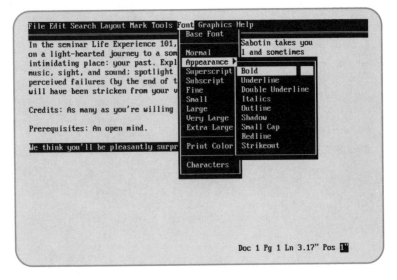

Figure 5-4. Choosing the **Bold** option.

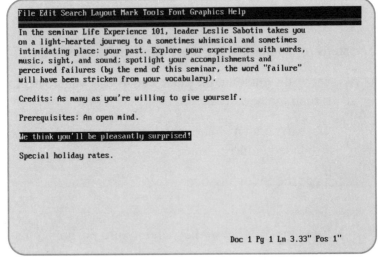

Figure 5-5. The document after the bold text has been added.

You can also change the look of text you've already typed. To do this, you select the text as a block and choose the options used in this lesson. (Lessons 10 and 11 explain selecting and working with blocks of text.)

In this lesson, you learned to underline and boldface the text in your document. The next lesson introduces you to WordPerfect's codes.

Lesson 6

Text Basics: Understanding WordPerfect Code

In this lesson, you'll learn to edit text enhancements by working with hidden codes.

Behind the normal WordPerfect screen, the program is keeping track of all the formatting and text changes you make by inserting invisible codes. For example, when you underlined text, WordPerfect added two codes: one that turned the underline feature on, and another that turned the feature off. Fortunately, WordPerfect allows you to see and edit these "invisible" codes on-screen.

Displaying Codes

You can display codes three different ways. With the seminar example document on the screen,

    1. Press F11.

      Or

    2. Press Alt-F3.

Or

3. Open the Edit menu and choose the Reveal Codes option.

About halfway down the screen, WordPerfect displays a copy of your document, complete with all the codes the program has entered for you. This is called the Reveal Codes screen. Your screen should look like Figure 6-1.

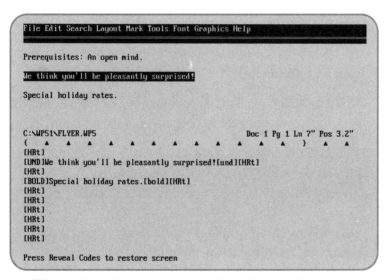

Figure 6-1. The codes in the WordPerfect document.

For many features, WordPerfect includes a pair of codes: one that turns the feature on, and another that turns the feature off. The [UND] code (for underline) is an example of this type of *paired code*. Other codes are known as *open codes*: these codes are placed in the text where you specify and remain in effect until another code replaces them or the end of the document is encountered. WordPerfect also uses *single codes*, such as [HRt] and [SRt] (for hard returns and soft returns), that simply record a code placed in the text at that specific location.

35

For a list of codes used throughout this book, see the List of Codes at the back of the book.

Editing Codes

You can edit, delete, or add codes while you are working in Reveal Codes. To do this, you simply move the cursor to the code you want to change and make the change as though you were working in the regular document. When you return to the document, WordPerfect records the change.

For example, you can remove the underline enhancement in your sample document by following these steps:

1. Press F11 (or Alt-F3) to reveal the codes. (Using the mouse, open the Edit menu and choose **Reveal Codes**).

2. Use the cursor keys to move the cursor in the Reveal Codes screen to the [UND] code.

3. Press Del.

WordPerfect removes *both* codes and returns to the normal text displayed in the document (see Figure 6-2).

Hiding Codes Again

You can hide codes three ways:

1. Press F11.

   Or

2. Press Alt-F3.

   Or

3. Press Alt to access the menu bar; then open the Edit menu and choose the **Reveal Codes** option.

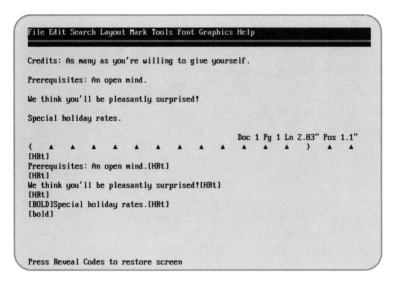

Figure 6-2. The Reveal Codes screen with [UND] codes removed.

WordPerfect returns you to a full-screen display of your document.

In this lesson, you've learned about WordPerfect's codes. In the next lesson, you'll learn to save the document you've created.

Lesson 7

Saving Your Work

In this lesson, you'll learn to save and name your WordPerfect documents.

Saving...The First Time

You can save as a file every WordPerfect document you create. When you're ready to save your document, follow these steps:

1. Open the File menu and choose **Save** or press F10 (Save).

   WordPerfect displays the message

   `Document to be saved:`

   You can then specify the drive, path, and name of the document you want to save.

Path The path you enter for a document is just what it sounds like—the path you tell WordPerfect to follow to save or retrieve a file. This path includes the drive (usually A:, B:, or C:) and the directory (and/or subdirectories).

2. After the `Document to be saved:` prompt, type the letter of the drive to which you are saving the file, followed by a colon. (If you are saving the file to a floppy disk in drive A, for example, you would enter A:).

3. If you are saving to a subdirectory, type a backslash (\), and then the name of the subdirectory. (A path can include several subdirectories. Be sure to include a backslash after every subdirectory name you type.)

4. Enter a name for the file you are saving. (*Note*: Naming tips are explained in the next section.)

5. Press Enter.

WordPerfect then saves the file on the drive and in the directory you specified.

Brushing Up on Directory Basics If the whole idea of working with drives and directories is confusing, consult *The First Book of MS-DOS* for information about working with directories.

Remember that even though you've saved the file once, you need to resave the file each time you make changes to the document. (This is explained later in this lesson.)

Naming Files

WordPerfect is easy to get along with when it comes to naming files. Most of the character keys on the keyboard can be used in file names.

WordPerfect allows you to use the following letters, characters, and symbols for your file names:

Characters A through Z (upper- or lowercase)

Numbers 0 through 9

The following symbols: ! @ # $ % ^ & ( ) - _

WordPerfect displays an error if you try to use names that include the following characters:

space ~ + = I \ / ? < > , { }

Invalid File Name What happens when you enter a file name WordPerfect doesn't like? Simply backspace through the name and type one that WordPerfect understands.

Performing Mini-Saves

If you make any changes to the document—tiny or otherwise—you need to save your work again.

When should you save a file? The answer to this is pretty open-ended: Every time you do anything significant to the file. As a general rule, remember to save your document after you do the following things:

- Enter large sections of text that you wouldn't want to re-enter

- Change format settings

- Make major modifications to the content or layout

- Retrieve another file into the current one

- Complete 15 to 30 minutes of work

To save the document after the initial save,

1. Open the File menu and choose Save or press F10 (Save).

2. When the `Document to be saved:` prompt appears, press Enter.

3. WordPerfect asks you whether you want to replace the existing file. Select **Yes**.

The file is then saved.

Saving Under Another Name When you are making major changes to a file, it's best to have a copy of the file you are changing, just in case you make changes you wish you hadn't made. Save another copy of the document by pressing F10 and entering a new file name.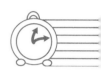

In this lesson, you learned to save and name your document files. The next lesson shows you how to retrieve files you've saved.

Lesson 8

Retrieving Your Document

In this lesson, you'll learn to load files you've saved.

Now that you know how to save your WordPerfect documents, you need to know how to open them again. This is known as *retrieving* files.

This section shows you three file retrieval situations:

- You know the drive, directory, and name of the file you want to retrieve

- You know the drive and directory but not the file name

- You have no idea whether you've found the right file or not and simply want to check by looking at its contents

Retrieving a Specific Document

When you know the drive, directory, and name of the file you want to retrieve, the procedure is simple:

1. Display a blank edit screen.

2. Open the File menu and choose **Retrieve** or press Shift-F10. WordPerfect then displays the `Document to be retrieved:` prompt.

3. Type the drive, path, and name of the file you want to retrieve.

4. Press Enter.

WordPerfect loads the document into RAM and displays it on your screen.

Displaying Directory Contents

When you don't know the name of the document you want to retrieve, you can enlist WordPerfect's help by using the List Files screen. Here are the steps:

1. When a blank edit screen is displayed, open the File menu and choose **List Files** or press F5 (List Files).

2. WordPerfect displays the drive and path of the current directory. (If you want to display the files in a different directory, enter the name of the directory you want to see, remembering to type a backslash between directories and subdirectories.)

3. Press Enter. WordPerfect then displays the List Files screen shown in Figure 8-1, listing all the files in the directory you specified.

4. Use the cursor keys to move the highlight to the file you want.

5. Press 1 to select the file.

WordPerfect then loads the file and displays it in the editing screen.

```
11-09-80  03:48p            Directory C:\WP51\*.*
Document size:    1,072   Free: 8,187,904 Used:  3,326,962     Files:    104

    .   Current    <Dir>                 ..    Parent     <Dir>
  8514A    .VRS     4,862  01-19-90 12:00p   ALTRNAT .WPK       919  01-19-90 12:00p
  ARROW-22.WPG        187  01-19-90 12:00p   ATI     .VRS     6,036  01-19-90 12:00p
  BALLOONS.WPG      3,187  01-19-90 12:00p   BANNER-3.WPG       719  01-19-90 12:00p
  BICYCLE .WPG        607  01-19-90 12:00p   BKGRND-1.WPG    11,391  01-19-90 12:00p
  BORDER-8.WPG        215  01-19-90 12:00p   BULB    .WPG     2,101  01-19-90 12:00p
  BURST-1 .WPG        819  01-19-90 12:00p   BUTTRFLY.WPG     5,349  01-19-90 12:00p
  CALENDAR.WPG        371  01-19-90 12:00p   CERTIF  .WPG       679  01-19-90 12:00p
  CHARACTR.DOC     43,029  01-19-90 12:00p   CHKBOX-1.WPG       653  01-19-90 12:00p
  CLOCK   .WPG      1,811  01-19-90 12:00p   CNTRCT-2.WPG     2,753  01-19-90 12:00p
  CODES   .WPM      7,403  01-19-90 12:00p   CONVERT .EXE   109,049  01-19-90 12:00p
  CURSOR  .COM      1,452  01-19-90 12:00p   DEVICE-2.WPG       657  01-19-90 12:00p
  DIPLOMA .WPG      2,413  01-19-90 12:00p   EGA512  .FRS     3,584  01-19-90 12:00p
  EGAITAL .FRS      3,584  01-19-90 12:00p   EGASMC  .FRS     3,584  01-19-90 12:00p
  EGAUND  .FRS      3,584  01-19-90 12:00p   EHANDLER.PS      2,797  11-06-89 12:00p
  ENDFOOT .WPM      3,871  01-19-90 12:00p   ENHANCED.WPK     3,571  01-19-90 12:00p
  EQUATION.WPK      2,974  01-19-90 12:00p   FIXBIOS .COM        50  01-19-90 12:00p
  FLOPPY-2.WPG        475  01-19-90 12:00p   FLYER   .WP5     1,064  11-09-80 03:47p
  FOOTEND .WPM      3,833  01-19-90 12:00p ▼ GAVEL   .WPG       887  01-19-90 12:00p

1 Retrieve; 2 Delete; 3 Move/Rename; 4 Print; 5 Short/Long Display;
6 Look; 7 Other Directory; 8 Copy; 9 Find; N Name Search: 6
```

Figure 8-1. The List Files screen.

Viewing a Document

There may be times when all the file names on the List File screen seem to run together—one looks the same as another. WordPerfect has a built-in "view" feature that allows you to see what's in a file without actually loading it. You can't edit when you are simply viewing a file, but you can determine whether you've found the file you need so that you can then retrieve the file and edit it as necessary.

To view a file, follow these steps:

1. Display a blank WordPerfect screen.

2. Open the File menu and choose List Files or press F5 (List Files).

3. Type the directory you want to display and press Enter.

4. Highlight the name of the file you want to view.

5. Press Enter. The document is then displayed on the screen.

6. Use the cursor keys to scroll through the text as necessary.

7. When you know whether this is the file you need or not, press F7 (Exit).

Retrieving a Viewed File After you view a file, you can retrieve it by simply pressing **1** when you return to the List Files screen.

Use the exit procedure to display a blank edit screen, if you already have a document retrieved and want to retrieve another. You can either save the first document or not, but do not exit the program.

Now that you know how to retrieve WordPerfect documents, you're ready to try your hand at seeing the fruits of your labor. The next lesson introduces you to printing.

Lesson 9

Previewing and Printing Your Work

In this lesson, you'll learn to preview and print your document.

Previewing the Document

When you want to see how your page will look in print, select the **View Document** option from the Print menu. Follow these steps:

1. Display the document you want to preview

2. Open the File menu and choose Print or press Shift-F7.

3. Type 6 to select View Document (see Figure 9-1).

WordPerfect then displays the document in *preview mode* on your screen. When you are ready to return to the document, press F7 (Exit).

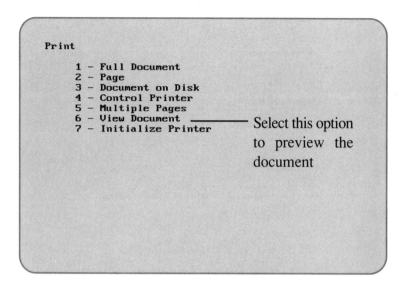

```
Print

    1 - Full Document
    2 - Page
    3 - Document on Disk
    4 - Control Printer
    5 - Multiple Pages
    6 - View Document ————————— Select this option
    7 - Initialize Printer          to preview the
                                    document
```

Figure 9-1. Previewing the document.

Preparing To Print

When you installed WordPerfect, you selected the type of printer (or printers) you would be using with the program. Before you can print, however, you still need to check the printer setup and make sure WordPerfect knows which printer it's going to use.

Checking the Printer Setup

To check the printer setup,

1. Open the File menu and choose **Print** or press Shift-F7.

2. From the Print menu (see Figure 9-2) type S to select the Select Printer option.

```
Print

    1 - Full Document
    2 - Page
    3 - Document on Disk
    4 - Control Printer
    5 - Multiple Pages
    6 - View Document
    7 - Initialize Printer


Options

    S - Select Printer                      QMS PS 810
    B - Binding Offset                      0"
    N - Number of Copies                    1
    U - Multiple Copies Generated by        WordPerfect
    G - Graphics Quality                    Medium
    T - Text Quality                        High



Selection: 0
```

Figure 9-2 The Print menu.

The Print: Select Printer screen is displayed, showing you the printer (or printers) you selected during installation (see Figure 9-3). You have the option of selecting a particular printer (if the one you plan to use is not highlighted, move the highlight to that printer and type **1**). If everything looks okay here, press F7 to escape out of this screen and return to the Print menu.

Initializing the Printer for Soft Fonts

If you are using a laser printer and soft fonts, you will need to initialize your printer before you print. The best time to initialize the printer is when you begin editing the document.

 Soft fonts Soft fonts are fonts—typefaces, styles, and sizes—that are stored on disk and sent to your printer at print time. Soft fonts are stored in your printer's internal memory.

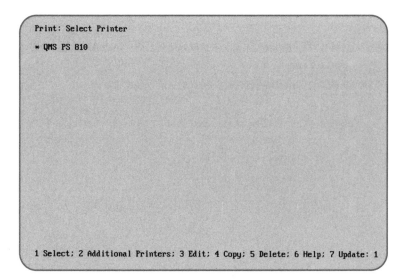

```
Print: Select Printer

* QMS PS 810
```

```
1 Select; 2 Additional Printers; 3 Edit; 4 Copy; 5 Delete; 6 Help; 7 Update: 1
```

Figure 9-3. The Print: Select Printer screen.

To initialize your printer for soft fonts,

1. Open the File menu.

2. Choose the **Print** option.

3. Type 7 to choose Initialize printer.

4. When prompted, press **Y**.

WordPerfect then sends the soft fonts to your printer. The light on the front of your printer may flash for several minutes while the computer is sending the information. Don't start another print operation until the printer light has finished flashing.

Using the Print Menu

The other items on the Print menu help you customize the printing process. If you want to print multiple copies, for example, you can type **N** to select **Number of copies** and then enter the number of copies you want to print. If you want to print from a disk rather than from the screen, you would select **3** (Document on Disk). Table 9-1 provides an overview of the options on the Print menu.

Table 9-1. Print Menu Options

Options	Description
Print	
1 - Full Document	Prints all of the current document
2 - Page	Prints current page only
3 - Document on Disk	Prints from a disk
4 - Control Printer	Controls speed and stops printing
5 - Multiple Pages	Prints selected pages of a document
6 - View Document	Previews document to be printed
7 - Initialize Printer	Sends soft fonts to printer
Options	
S - Select Printer	Allows you to check printer setup or select a different printer
B - Binding Offset	Lets you add extra space to the inside margin to allow for binding or hole punching
N - Number of Copies	Allows you to specify number of copies printed
U - Multiple Copies Generated by	Specifies whether your printer, WordPerfect, or your network is responsible for generating multiple copies

Table 9-1. (continued)

Options	Description
G - Graphics Quality	Controls quality of printed graphics
T - Text Quality	Controls quality of printed text

Printing the Document

To print your document, follow these simple steps:

1. Display the document you want to print.

2. Open the File menu and choose **Print**.

3. Type 1.

WordPerfect chugs for just a moment and then your printer should leap into life.

In the next lesson, we'll get back into the document and work with blocks (of text).

Selecting Blocks of Text

In this lesson, you'll learn how to select a block of text.

Understanding Text Blocks

A text block is any text—from one character to an entire document—that you highlight in order to perform certain operations, such as copying, moving, or deleting. For example, if you want to copy a paragraph, you must first mark the paragraph as a block before you try to copy it; otherwise, WordPerfect won't know what you want to copy.

Other operations that require that you mark a block first include

- Moving text

- Deleting text (more than one character, word, or line)

- Saving portions of text

- Printing individual paragraphs from a larger document

- Changing the format for a portion of a document

- Changing the font of a specific phrase within a paragraph

Marking Text Blocks

Let's return to the example we've been using throughout. The document currently looks like Figure 10-1.

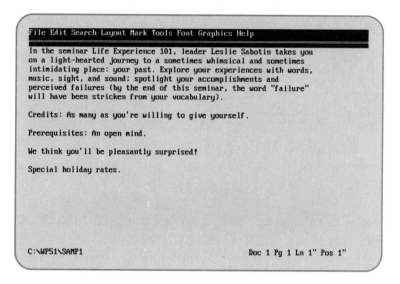

File Edit Search Layout Mark Tools Font Graphics Help

In the seminar Life Experience 101, leader Leslie Sabotin takes you on a light-hearted journey to a sometimes whimsical and sometimes intimidating place: your past. Explore your experiences with words, music, sight, and sound; spotlight your accomplishments and perceived failures (by the end of this seminar, the word "failure" will have been stricken from your vocabulary).

Credits: As many as you're willing to give yourself.

Prerequisites: An open mind.

We think you'll be pleasantly surprised!

Special holiday rates.

C:\WP51\SAMP1   Doc 1 Pg 1 Ln 1" Pos 1"

Figure 10-1. The sample document.

To highlight the first paragraph, follow these steps:

1. Move the cursor to the first character in the paragraph.

2. Open the Edit menu.

3. Select the **Block** option. WordPerfect displays the message *Block on* in the bottom left corner of the screen (see Figure 10-2).

4. Press Enter to highlight to the end of the paragraph.

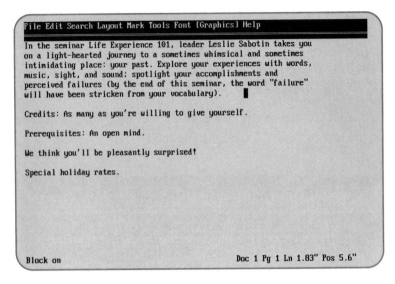

```
File Edit Search Layout Mark Tools Font [Graphics] Help

In the seminar Life Experience 101, leader Leslie Sabotin takes you
on a light-hearted journey to a sometimes whimsical and sometimes
intimidating place: your past. Explore your experiences with words,
music, sight, and sound; spotlight your accomplishments and
perceived failures (by the end of this seminar, the word "failure"
will have been stricken from your vocabulary).  ▌

Credits: As many as you're willing to give yourself.

Prerequisites: An open mind.

We think you'll be pleasantly surprised!

Special holiday rates.




Block on                              Doc 1 Pg 1 Ln 1.83" Pos 5.6"
```

Figure 10-2. Marking a block of text.

Marking a Section of Text

You won't always be marking entire paragraphs as blocks of text; sometimes you'll need only a few words or lines. To mark a section of text, you have different procedures, depending on whether you use the mouse or the keyboard.

If you're using a mouse,

1. Position the cursor where you want to begin the block.

2. Press the left mouse button and, while holding the button down, drag the mouse until the block you want is highlighted.

3. Release the mouse button.

WordPerfect highlights the block and you can now copy, move, save, or print it as necessary (see Figure 10-3).

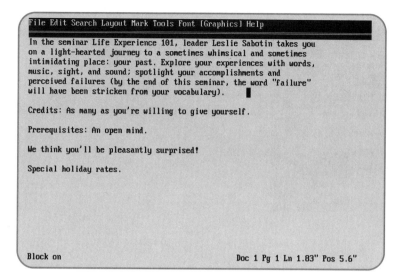

File Edit Search Layout Mark Tools Font [Graphics] Help

In the seminar Life Experience 101, leader Leslie Sabotin takes you
on a light-hearted journey to a sometimes whimsical and sometimes
intimidating place: your past. Explore your experiences with words,
music, sight, and sound; spotlight your accomplishments and
perceived failures (by the end of this seminar, the word "failure"
will have been stricken from your vocabulary).

Credits: As many as you're willing to give yourself.

Prerequisites: An open mind.

We think you'll be pleasantly surprised!

Special holiday rates.

Block on   Doc 1 Pg 1 Ln 1.83" Pos 5.6"

Figure 10-3. The marked text block.

If you're using the keyboard,

1. Use the cursor movement keys to position the cursor at the place where you want the highlight to begin.

2. Press Alt to move to the menu bar.

3. Open the Edit menu and choose Block (see Figure 10-4).

4. Use the cursor keys to move the cursor to the point you want the block to end.

WordPerfect then marks the block and you can work with it as necessary.

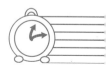

Marking Text Blocks When you want to mark a block of text, you can bypass the menu selections by pressing Alt-F4 or F12 to turn highlighting on.

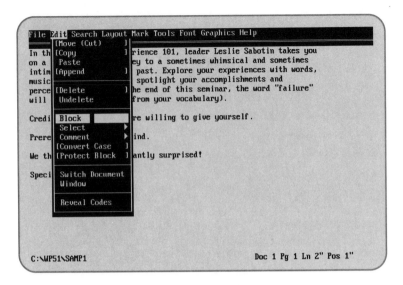

Figure 10-4. Selecting the **Block** option.

In this lesson, you learned to mark a block of text. The next lesson shows you how to work with the text you've marked.

Working with Blocks of Text

In this lesson, you'll learn to copy, move, delete, save, append, and print text blocks.

Copying Text Blocks

When you want to copy a block of text, follow these steps:

1. Mark the block you want to copy.

2. Open the Edit menu.

3. Select the Copy option (see Figure 11-1). WordPerfect makes a copy of the block and places the copy on an unseen clipboard.

4. When WordPerfect prompts you to `Move cursor; press Enter to retrieve,` use the cursor keys to move the cursor after the first paragraph; then press Enter.

WordPerfect then places the copied block at the position you indicated.

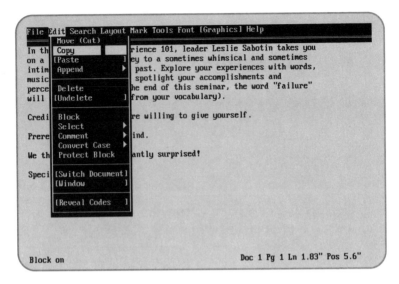

Figure 11-1. Selecting the **Copy** option.

Moving Text Blocks

When you want to move a block of text, follow these steps:

1. Mark the block you want to move.

2. Open the Edit menu.

3. Choose the Move option (see Figure 11-2). WordPerfect places the block on the clipboard.

4. Move the cursor to the point to which you want the block to be moved.

5. Press Enter.

WordPerfect then places the block at the position you specified.

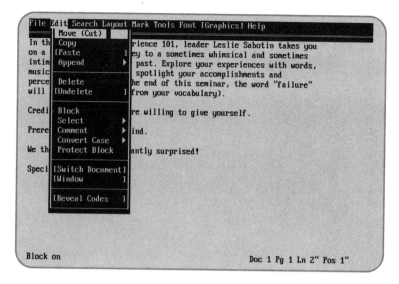

Figure 11-2. Choosing the **Move** option.

Deleting Text Blocks

To delete a block of text, follow these steps:

1. Mark the block to be deleted.

2. Open the Edit menu.

3. Choose the Delete option (see Figure 11-3).

4. When WordPerfect asks `Delete Block? No (Yes)`, type **Y**.

WordPerfect then deletes the marked block.

Uh-oh... If you just deleted something and got that all-too-familiar "omigosh-I-needed-that" feeling, you can recover the last thing you deleted by pressing F1 (Cancel) or opening the Edit menu and choosing the **Undelete** option.

59

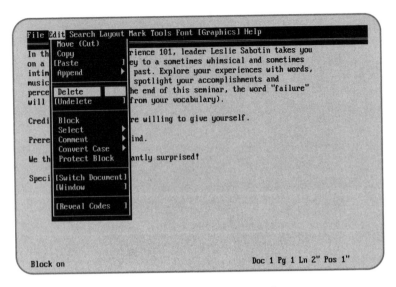

Figure 11-3. Selecting the **Delete** option.

Saving Text Blocks

WordPerfect gives you the option of saving out a portion—a block—of your document. To save a text block out as a separate file, follow these steps:

1. Mark the block you want to save.

2. Open the File menu.

3. Select the Save option (see Figure 11-4).

4. When WordPerfect displays the prompt Block name:, type a name for the block.

5. Press Enter.

Saving a Marked Block You can shortcut the menu-selection route to saving a marked block by pressing F10, entering a file name, and pressing Enter.

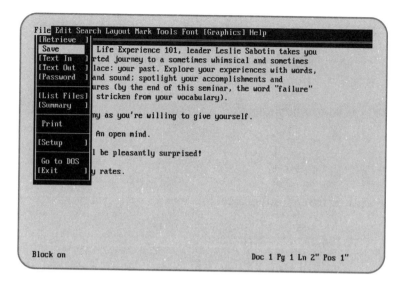

Figure 11-4. Saving a marked block.

Appending Text Blocks

WordPerfect gives you yet another block-manipulation option: You can also add blocks of text to files you've already created. To save the text block and add (or *append*) it to another file, follow these steps:

1. Mark the block you want to append.

2. Open the Edit menu.

3. Choose the **Append** option.

4. Choose the **To File** option.

5. When WordPerfect asks for the name of the file to which you want to append the block, type the file name and press Enter. WordPerfect then appends the block to the end of the file you specified.

Printing Text Blocks

You may also want to print only a section of text. To print a text block, follow these steps:

1. Mark the block you want to print.

2. Open the File menu.

3. Select **Print**.

4. When WordPerfect asks you `Print block?`, type **Y**. If your printer is connected properly and is on-line, the block is then printed.

This lesson showed you various methods of working with text blocks. The next lesson further expands your text manipulation talents by teaching you about WordPerfect's search and replace feature.

Lesson 12

Searching and Replacing Text

In this lesson, you'll learn to use WordPerfect's search and replace feature to edit your documents.

What Is Search and Replace?

WordPerfect's search and replace feature allows you to find a word or phrase in your document and replace it with something else.

You might use the search and replace feature, for example, in the following cases:

- When a late-breaking change affects a name or term used frequently in your document

- When you need to search for certain characters

- When you need to move quickly to a specific place in the document (in this case you would use only search—not search and replace)

Searching for Text

When using search and replace, you have the option of selecting the following things:

- Which direction you want to search (forward—from the front of the document to back; or backward—from the end of the document to the front)

- Whether you want to search for entire words or parts of words

- Whether you want to search for text, headers and footers, endnotes, or graphics boxes

- Whether you want to search for hidden codes

Forward Searching

To search your document from the beginning to the end:

1. Move the cursor to the place you want to begin the search.

2. Open the Search menu.

3. Choose the Forward option (see Figure 12-1).

4. When WordPerfect displays the `-> Srch:` prompt, type the text you want to search for.

5. Press F2 (Search). WordPerfect then searches for and moves the cursor to the first occurrence of the text you specified.

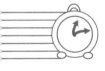

Searching Headers and Footers If the text you are searching for isn't in the regular text of the document (that is, the text is in a header, footer, or another element separate from the body text), you can perform an extended search by pressing Home-F2 (or by opening the Search menu and choosing **Extended** and then **Forward**).

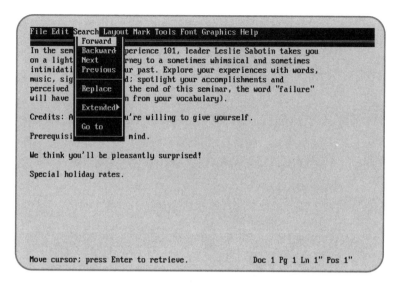

File Edit Search Layout Mark Tools Font Graphics Help
```
              | Forward  |
In the sem   | Backward |perience 101, leader Leslie Sabotin takes you
on a light   | Next     |rney to a sometimes whimsical and sometimes
intimidati   | Previous |ur past. Explore your experiences with words,
music, sig   |          |d; spotlight your accomplishments and
perceived    | Replace  | the end of this seminar, the word "failure"
will have    |          |n from your vocabulary).
             | Extended▶|
Credits: A   |          |u're willing to give yourself.
             | Go to    |
Prerequisi   |          |mind.

We think you'll be pleasantly surprised!

Special holiday rates.



Move cursor; press Enter to retrieve.          Doc 1 Pg 1 Ln 1" Pos 1"
```

Figure 12-1. Selecting the **Forward** option.

Backward Searching

To search backward through the document, follow these steps:

1. Move the cursor to the place you want to begin the search.

2. Open the Search menu.

3. Choose the Backward option.

4. When WordPerfect displays the `<- Srch:` prompt, type the text you want to search for.

5. Press F2 (Search). WordPerfect then searches for and moves the cursor to the text you specified.

Using Wild Cards in a Search

When you're using the search and replace feature, a wild-card character can be used in place of other letters.

To use a wild card in the search, follow these steps:

1. Position the cursor at the beginning of the document.

2. When the prompt is displayed, type the portion of the word you know how to spell; then, at the part you're unsure of, press Ctrl-V and then Ctrl-X. WordPerfect places a ^X symbol in the word on the Srch: line. Then enter the rest of the word (see Figure 12-2).

3. Press F2 to begin the search.

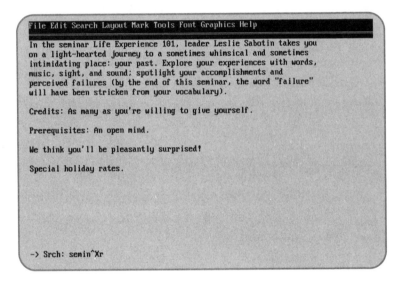

Figure 12-2. Using wild cards in a search.

WordPerfect then moves the cursor to the first occurrence of the word you specified.

Searching for Hidden Codes

WordPerfect enables you not only to search the text in your document, but also to search the hidden codes in the document.

Follow these steps to search for a code:

1. Go to the beginning of the document.

2. Press F2.

3. At the `-> Srch:` prompt, press the key or key combination that inserted the code.

4. Press F2.

WordPerfect then searches for and finds the code you specified.

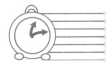

Searching for Codes It is not necessary to reveal codes when you are searching for them in your WordPerfect document, but you may find it helpful to see where you're going. To turn on (and, later, to turn off) Reveal Codes, press Alt-F3.

Replacing Text

In many cases, the search procedure goes hand-in-hand with a replace procedure. WordPerfect enables you to search for specific text and replace the text with something else— whether it's one word or several.

You can choose whether you want to search and replace an item throughout an entire document or only at selective occurrences.

Selective Replacing

WordPerfect gives you the option of choosing when you want to use search and replace. To replace only selected text, follow these steps:

1. Open the Search menu.

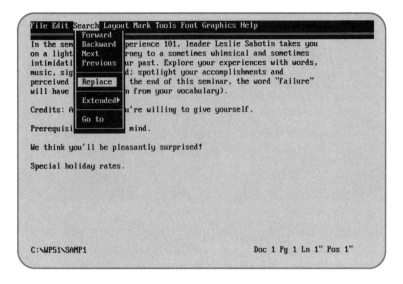

Figure 12-3. Selecting the **Replace** option.

2. Choose the Replace option (see Figure 12-3).

3. When WordPerfect displays the prompt w/Con-firm? No (Yes), type Y. (This tells WordPerfect that you want to confirm the replacement.)

4. After the Srch: prompt, type the text you want to search for and press F2.

5. When the Replace with: prompt is displayed, type the text you want to insert.

6. Press F2.

7. When w/Confirm? is displayed again, press Y to confirm the replacement or N to skip it.

WordPerfect will stop each time the text you are searching for is found and ask whether you want to replace it.

Searching and Replacing You can bypass the menu selections by pressing Alt-F2 to begin the search and replace procedure.

Global Replacing

In some cases, you'll want to find every place a word or phrase is used and replace it. This is known as *global replacing*. This time, try using the speed key instead of the menus. Follow these steps to do a global search and replace:

1. Press Alt-F2 (Replace).

2. When WordPerfect displays the prompt w/Con-firm? No (Yes), type N. (This tells WordPerfect that, after you start the search, you want the program to go ahead and make the change without asking for confirmation.)

3. After the Srch: prompt, type the text you want to replace and press F2.

4. When the Replace with: prompt is displayed, type the text you want to insert.

5. Press F2.

Now that you've been through some of the editing features of WordPerfect, you're ready to begin working with the way you place text on the page. The next lesson begins this topic with a look at selecting paper size and setting margins.

Selecting Paper Size and Setting Margins

In this lesson, you'll learn to select paper size and set the top, bottom, left, and right margins of your document.

The *margin* of your document is the amount of white space WordPerfect leaves between your text and the edge of the page. Because the amount of white space you want around your document may depend, in part, on the size of the page you use, you should get into the habit of selecting the paper size for your document before you set or modify margins. (You can do either first, however.)

When you are working with paper size and margins, you use the options available in the Format: Page menu (see Figure 13-1). The sections that follow explain each of these procedures.

Choosing Paper Size and Type

When you first begin using WordPerfect, the program assumes that you are using 8 1/2-by-11-inch paper. If you are using basic office stationery or computer paper, this default setting is usually fine.

```
Format: Page

     1 - Center Page (top to bottom)      No

     2 - Force Odd/Even Page

     3 - Headers

     4 - Footers

     5 - Margins - Top                    1"
                   Bottom                 1"

     6 - Page Numbering

     7 - Paper Size                       8.5" x 11"
                   Type                   Standard

     8 - Suppress (this page only)



Selection: 0
```

Figure 13-1. The Format: Page menu.

To select a new paper size and type, follow these steps:

1. Open the Layout menu and choose the **Page** option.

2. When the Format:Page menu is displayed, type **7** to select Paper Size/Type.

3. When the Format:Paper Size/Type menu is displayed, highlight the paper selection you want, press **1** (see Figure 13-2) and press F7.

Working with Custom Paper Sizes WordPerfect gives you the option of entering your own paper sizes. If you have an unusual paper size, type **o** (for *Other*) in place of the number. Then, type the dimensions of the page—width first, and then height.

Working with Margins

WordPerfect gives you four margins to deal with—top, bottom, right, and left. All these settings may be the same (they are all preset to 1 inch), or you may want to change them so that, for example, the top margin allows more space than the bottom.

```
Format: Paper Size/Type
                                                      Font  Double
Paper type and Orientation     Paper Size     Prompt Loc    Type  Sided  Labels

Envelope - Wide                9.5" x 4"      Yes    Manual  Land  No
Standard                       8.5" x 11"     No     Contin  Port  No
Standard - Wide                11" x 8.5"     No     Contin  Land  No
[ALL OTHERS]                   Width ≤ 8.5"   Yes    Manual        No




 1 Select; 2 Add; 3 Copy; 4 Delete; 5 Edit; N Name Search: 1
```

Figure 13-2. The Format: Paper Size/Type menu.

Setting Top and Bottom Margins

When you want to modify the top and bottom margins follow these steps:

1. Place the cursor at the top of the document.

2. Press Alt; then open the Layout menu.

3. Select the Page option.

4. Type 5 to select Margins Top and Bottom.

5. Type the size of the margin you want in inches for the top.

6. Press Enter.

7. Type the margin setting for the bottom.

8. Press Enter.

9. Press F7 (Exit).

Margin Codes Remember that WordPerfect inserts codes in the document when you perform certain operations and press certain keys. (You can display the codes by pressing Alt-F3.) When you change the margin settings, WordPerfect inserts a code at that point in the document. If you later want to change the margin, you can display the code and edit the code on the screen rather than adding new margin settings.

Setting Left and Right Margins

To change the left and right margins in your document, follow these steps:

1. Place the cursor at the point you want to change the margins.

2. Open the Layout menu.

3. Choose the **Line** option.

4. Type 7 to select Margins Left/Right.

5. Type the size of margin you want in inches for the left margin.

6. Press Enter.

7. Type the margin setting for the right margin.

8. Press Enter.

9. Press F7 (Exit).

WordPerfect then records the margins you set and will place the text accordingly.

This lesson showed you how to choose paper size and type and work with the margins for your document. The next lesson explains working with tabs.

Working with Tabs

In this lesson, you'll learn how to add and work with different types of tabs in your WordPerfect document.

Using Tabs

WordPerfect offers four different types of tabs that let you move quickly across the screen and set the vertical alignment of columns with numbers or text:

- Left tabs
- Right tabs
- Center tabs
- Decimal tabs

You use a left tab when you want to vertically align a column of text along the left edge; a right tab to align a column along the right edge; a center tab when you want to center-align a column; and a decimal tab when you want to align a column of numbers on the decimal point (see Figure 14-1).

```
File Edit Search Layout Mark Tools Font Graphics Help


    Class               Date  Instructor        Cost

    Life Experiences    01/23/91    Sabotin       75.00
    Parenting           01/30/91    Murray        50.00
    Writing Seminar     02/23/91    Marshall      35.00
    Visualization       02/28/91    Sabotin       50.00
    Dreaming Awake      03/15/91    Reed          60.00










C:\WP51\SAMP1                            Doc 1 Pg 1 Ln 1.33" Pos 3.9"
```

Figure 14-1. A list using left, right, center, and decimal tabs.

WordPerfect has preset tabs every half inch across your document. Use the Tab key to move the cursor to the next tab position.

Try it with the example document. Display the document on-screen, then

- Press Tab four times.

Each time you press the Tab key, the cursor moves to the next tab position. To move back,

- Press Backspace four times.

Displaying the Tab Line

To display a ruler line showing where the default tabs are placed, follow these steps:

1. Open the Layout menu or press Shift-F8(Format).

2. Select **Line** or type **1**. The Format:Line menu is displayed at the bottom of the screen (see Figure 14-2).

3. Type **8** to select Tab Set.

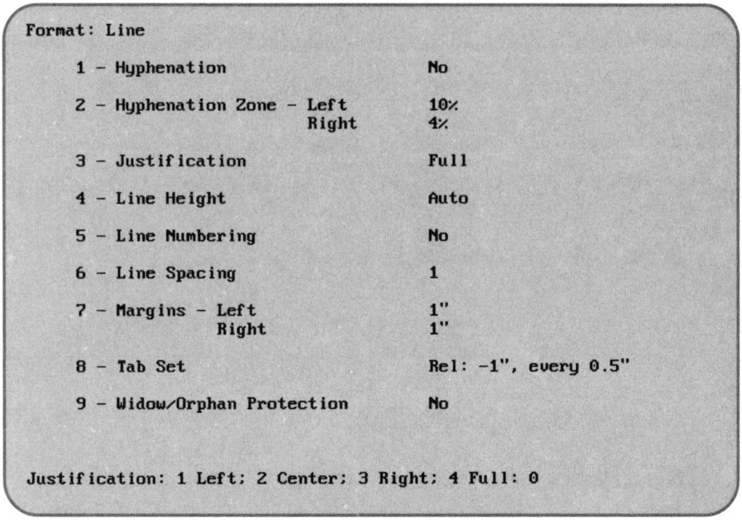

```
Format: Line

    1 - Hyphenation                  No

    2 - Hyphenation Zone - Left      10%
                          Right      4%

    3 - Justification                Full

    4 - Line Height                  Auto

    5 - Line Numbering               No

    6 - Line Spacing                 1

    7 - Margins - Left               1"
                  Right              1"

    8 - Tab Set                      Rel: -1", every 0.5"

    9 - Widow/Orphan Protection      No


Justification: 1 Left; 2 Center; 3 Right; 4 Full: 0
```

Figure 14-2. The Format: Line menu.

The tab line is then displayed at the bottom of the screen. A left tab is marked by an L on the line, a right tab by an R, a center tab by a C, and a decimal tab by a D. In the default tabs, shown in the tab lines in Figure 14-3, all the tabs are left tabs.

Clearing Tabs

Depending on the number of tabs you want in your document, you may want to clear out the tabs that are preset in WordPerfect. To do so follow these steps:

1. Display the tab line.

2. Use the arrow keys to move the cursor to the tab you want to clear.

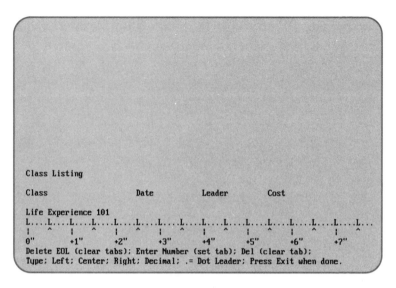

Figure 14-3. The default left tabs on the tab line.

3. Press Backspace or Del.

WordPerfect then removes the tabs.

Clearing All Tabs—the Quick Way If you want to clear all the tabs in your WordPerfect document, you can take a shortcut. First, press Home, Home, and the left-arrow key. Then press Ctrl-End.

Setting Tabs

The procedure is the same for setting the different types of tabs. Only the final option you select differs. Just follow these steps:

1. Open the Layout menu (or press Shift-F8).

2. Choose Line or type 1 to select Line.

3. When the Format: Line menu is displayed, select 8 Tab Set.

4. The tab line is then displayed along the bottom of the screen. Use the arrow keys to move the cursor to the point you want to add the tab.

5. Type L to set a left tab, R to set a right tab, C to set a center tab, or D to set a decimal tab.

6. Add any other tabs you want; then press F7 (Exit) twice to return to the document.

If Your Tabs Aren't Working Properly... Check Reveal Codes (Alt-F3) to see if you've accidentally placed extra tab settings in the text. Delete any unneccessary tabs. If the tabs you've set seem to have no effect, perhaps the cursor was positioned below the text you wanted to tab when you set the tabs. Move the cursor to a point in the document before the place you want to tab the text and reset the tabs.

Moving Tabs

Moving a tab is really nothing more than clearing the tab and adding another one at the point you want.

1. Press Shift-F8 (Format) and select 1 Line to display the Format: Line menu.

2. Select 8 Tab Set.

3. On the tab line, use the arrow keys to move the cursor to the tab you want to move.

4. Press Del.

5. Use the arrow keys to move to the place you want to add the tab.

6. Type the letter of the tab you want to add (**L** for left, **R** for right, **C** for center, or **D** for decimal).

7. Press F7 (Exit) twice to return to the document.

Dealing with Multiple Tabs... It's not necessary to use Reveal Codes (Alt-F3) or the preceding steps to cancel tabs when you want to change a tab setting; you can simply add another tab at the point you want it to take effect.

Adding Dot Leaders

In setting every tab type except center tabs, WordPerfect gives you the option of including leaders in your tabbed material. *Leaders* are dots that WordPerfect inserts when you press Tab. Dot leaders "lead" the reader's eye from the beginning of text to the text at the tab stop. You would use dot leaders, for example, when creating a table of contents (see Figure 14-4).

To add a tab with dot leaders in your document, follow these steps:

1. Press Shift-F8 (Format) and select **1** Line to display the Format: Line menu.

2. Select **8** Tab Set.

3. On the tab line, use the arrow keys to move the cursor to the place you want to add the tab with leaders.

4. Type the letter of the tab you want to add (**L** for left, **R** for right, or **D** for decimal).

5. Type a period.

6. Press F7 (Exit) twice to return to the document.

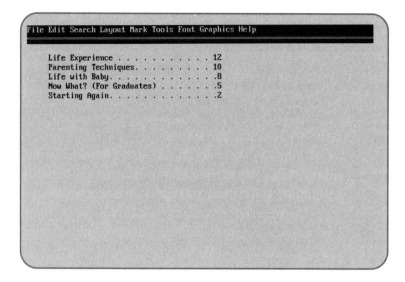

Figure 14-4. Using tabs with dot leaders.

Now each time you press Tab to move the cursor to that tab stop, WordPerfect adds dot leaders in the document.

In this lesson, you've learned to display the default tabs. You've also learned to clear, set, and change the tabs in your document. In the next lesson, you'll work with the alignment of text.

Lesson 15

Aligning Your Text

In this lesson, you'll learn to align your text by working with indents and text justification.

Indenting Text

WordPerfect gives you several options for indenting text in your documents:

- Left indents, where the text is indented from the left margin only

- Left and right indents, where the text is indented from both the left and right margins

- Hanging indents, where the first line of text is placed at the left margin and all subsequent lines in that paragraph are indented

Figure 15-1 shows the sample document with an example of left, left and right, and hanging indents. The following sections explain the procedures for using each of these indent types.

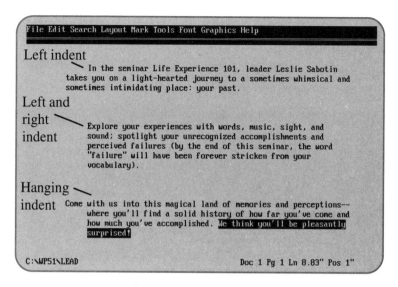

Figure 15-1. An example of indents.

Setting a Left Indent

To set a left indent, follow these steps:

1. Place the cursor at the start of the line where you want to begin the indented text.

2. Press F4 (Left Indent). WordPerfect moves the cursor to the next tab stop.

3. Type the text.

4. Press Enter.

Indenting Left and Right

To set a left and right indent for your document, follow these steps:

1. Position the cursor at the start of the line you want to indent.

2. Press Shift-F4 (Left/Right Indent). WordPerfect moves the cursor to the next tab stop from the left edge of the screen and automatically moves the indent from the right edge inward one tab.

3. Type the text you want to indent.

4. Press Enter.

Setting a Hanging Indent

A hanging indent is different than other indents, because the first line is actually "outdented;" that is, the first line of the text begins at the left margin and all subsequent lines in that paragraph are indented (refer back to Figure 15-1 for an example of a hanging indent).

To set a hanging indent in your text, follow these steps:

1. Place the cursor on the line where you want to begin the hanging indent.

2. Press F4 (Left Indent).

3. Press Shift-Tab (Margin Release).

4. Type the text for the hanging indent.

5. Press Enter.

Changing Indention Levels You control how far WordPerfect indents the text by repeatedly pressing F4 or Shift-F4 (depending on which indent you are using—left or left and right).

WordPerfect leaves the first line at the left margin and indents other wrap-around lines in that paragraph to the indent you specified.

Indenting Existing Text

Each time you press F4 or Shift-F4 to indent text, WordPerfect places an indent code in your document. To indent existing text, press F4 or Shift-F4 to add the indent code at the beginning of the text block you want to indent. Then, when you use the down-arrow key to move through the block. WordPerfect automatically reforms the text.

Controlling Justification

WordPerfect also allows you to control the justification of your text. *Justification* is a somewhat cryptic word for the alignment of your text. WordPerfect gives you the option of aligning your text in the following ways:

- Left justified, where the text lines up along the left margin and has a ragged (non-aligned) right margin

- Right justified, where the text lines up along the right margin and has a ragged left margin

- Full justified, where the text is lined up evenly along the left and right margins

- Centered, where the text is centered between the left and right margins

Figure 15-2 shows an example of each type of justification. By default, WordPerfect automatically places your text in left justified format. To change that justification (or to change back to the default from a different justification), follow these steps:

1. Place the cursor at the start of the line where you want the new justification to begin.

2. Open the Layout menu or press Shift-F8 (Format).

```
File Edit Search Layout Mark Tools Font Graphics Help


        In the seminar Life Experience 101, leader Leslie Sabotin
    takes you on a light-hearted journey to a sometimes whimsical and
    sometimes intimidating place: your past.


    Explore your experiences with words, music, sight, and sound;
        spotlight your unrecognized accomplishments and perceived
    failures (by the end of this seminar, the word "failure" will
                have been forever stricken from your vocabulary).

    Come with us into this magical land of memories and perceptions-
    -where you'll find a solid history of how far you've come and how
    much you've accomplished. We think you'll be pleasantly surprised!


        In the seminar Life Experience 101, leader
                Leslie Sabotin takes you on a
        light-hearted journey to a sometimes whimsical and sometimes
                    intimidating place: your past.

 C:\WP51\LEAD                            Doc 1 Pg 1 Ln 8.5" Pos 3.5"
```

Figure 15-2. Samples of text justification.

3. Select **Line** or type **1**.

4. When the Format: Line menu is displayed, press **3** to choose the Justification option (see Figure 15-3).

5. Type one of the following numbers to select justification:

    1 Left justified
    2 Centered
    3 Right justified
    4 Full justified

6. Press F7 (Exit) to return to the document.

If you want to cancel the justification, you can either delete the code (by using Alt-F3 to reveal the codes and deleting the code manually) or select a different type of justification by using the procedure just described.

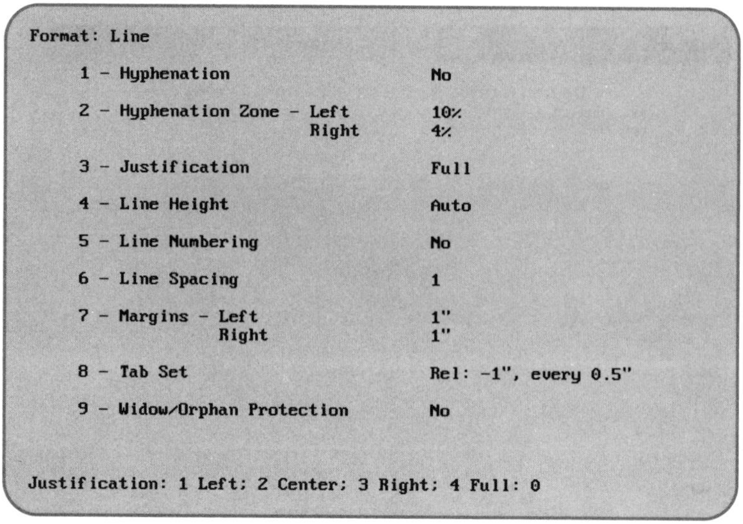

```
Format: Line

    1 - Hyphenation                        No

    2 - Hyphenation Zone - Left            10%
                           Right           4%

    3 - Justification                      Full

    4 - Line Height                        Auto

    5 - Line Numbering                     No

    6 - Line Spacing                       1

    7 - Margins - Left                     1"
                  Right                    1"

    8 - Tab Set                            Rel: -1", every 0.5"

    9 - Widow/Orphan Protection            No


Justification: 1 Left; 2 Center; 3 Right; 4 Full: 0
```

Figure 15-3. The Format: Line menu.

Working with Line Spacing

When you begin working with WordPerfect, the program
assumes that you want the text single-spaced. You have the
option, however, of double- or triple-spacing your text; in
fact, WordPerfect will allow you to insert as many blank lines
as you wish between the lines of text in your document.

To change the line spacing in your document, follow these
steps:

1. Position the cursor at the point you want to change the
   line spacing.

2. Open the Layout menu or press Shift-F8 (Format).

3. Type **1** to select Line.

4. At the Format: Line menu, type **6** to choose the Line
   Spacing option.

5. Enter the number of blank lines you want inserted between text lines.

6. Press Enter.

7. Press F7 (Exit) to return to the document.

WordPerfect then adds an unseen code to the document at that point, and the new line spacing goes into effect. (You can see the code by pressing Alt-F3 to reveal the codes, if you wish.)

This lesson has introduced you to controlling the placement and alignment of your text, using indents, justification, and line spacing options. The next lesson shows you how to use fonts to change the look of your text.

Working with Fonts

In this lesson, you'll learn to select and change the fonts in your WordPerfect document and to change the look of the text by modifying the text style.

What Are Fonts?

Put simply, a *font* is one size and style of a particular type family (also called a *typeface*). One font you might use could be Helvetica 10-point bold. In this example, *Helvetica* is the typeface, *10-point* is the size, and *bold* is the style.

Determining Your Printer's Font Capability

The fonts available to you will depend on the type of printer you are using. Before you use fonts in your documents, you need to find out what your particular printer is capable of printing. Follow these steps:

1. Open the Font menu or press Ctrl-F8 (Font).

2. Select the **Base Font** option or type **4**.

The Base Font screen is then displayed, showing you a list of the fonts available for the printer you've installed (see Figure 16-1). Your list may vary from the one shown here, depending on the printer you are using.

```
Base Font

 * Courier
   Courier Bold
   Courier Bold Oblique
   Courier Oblique
   Helvetica
   Helvetica Bold
   Helvetica Bold Oblique
   Helvetica Narrow
   Helvetica Narrow Bold
   Helvetica Narrow Bold Oblique
   Helvetica Narrow Oblique
   Helvetica Oblique
   ITC Avant Garde Gothic Book
   ITC Avant Garde Gothic Book Oblique
   ITC Avant Garde Gothic Demi
   ITC Avant Garde Gothic Demi Oblique
   ITC Bookman Demi
   ITC Bookman Demi Italic
   ITC Bookman Light
   ITC Bookman Light Italic
   ITC Zapf Chancery Medium Italic

 1 Select; N Name search: 1
```

Figure 16-1. The Base Font screen for a PostScript laser printer.

Selecting Fonts

Now you can choose a different font for your text, if you wish. To choose a new base font,

1. Use the arrow keys or the mouse to move the highlight to the font you want to use.

2. Type 1 to choose the Select option or double-click the left mouse button.

WordPerfect then inserts a [Font:] code in the text at the cursor position; this code affects all subsequent text up to the next [Font:] code. (If you want the entire document to print in the new font, move the cursor to the beginning of the document before you press Ctrl-F8.)

Changing the Font of Selected Text

There will be times when you want to change the font of a selected portion of text. You may want to actually change the typeface, or you may just want to change the size or style of the base font.

Changing the Font for a Text Block

To change the font used in a portion of text, follow these steps:

1. Move the cursor to the beginning of the block you want to change.

2. Open the Font menu or press Ctrl-F8 (Font).

3. Choose Base Font or type 4.

4. Use the arrow keys or the mouse to select the font you want to use.

5. Press Enter.

6. Move the cursor to the end of the block, and repeat steps 2-4 to select the original font.

   WordPerfect then places the marked block in the font you specified.

Changing Type Size

The procedure for changing the size of the type for a selected portion of text is slightly different than changing the base font. WordPerfect gives you the following options for choosing the size of text:

91

- Fine

- Small

- Large

- Very large

- Extra large

- Superscript

- Subscript

To change the size of type for a selected block of text, follow these steps:

1. Move the cursor to the beginning of the block you want to change.

2. Press Alt-F4 and highlight the block.

3. Open the Font menu or press Ctrl-F8 (Font) and type 1.

4. Select the size you want to use.

5. Press Enter.

WordPerfect changes the block you specified to the new size.

Changing Text Style

WordPerfect gives you several options for enhancing the look of the typeface you've chosen, including

- Bold

- Underline

- Double underline

- Italic

- Outline

- Shadow

- Small caps

- Redline

- Strikeout

Not all printers can print the more specialized styles such as small caps, shadow, and outline. You may need to experiment with the different styles to see which ones you can produce.

To change the type style in your document, follow these steps:

1. Move the cursor to the beginning of the block you want to change.

2. Press Alt-F4 and highlight the block.

3. Open the Font menu or press Ctrl-F8 (Font).

4. Choose **Appearance** or type **2**.

5. Select the type style you want to use.

6. Press Enter.

WordPerfect then places the codes that begin and end the type style at the beginning and end of the block you marked. If you want to remove the type style, you can press Alt-F3 and then delete either of the codes; both codes disappear.

Changing the Look of Text before You Enter It

If you want to type a section of text in a different size or style, follow these steps:

1. Position the cursor at the point you want to insert the text.

2. Open the Font menu or press Ctrl-F8 (Font).

3. If you're using the pull-down menu, select the style you want from the displayed list. From the Font menu, select the number of the item you want to change (1 for Size, 2 for Appearance).

4. Type the text, and press the right-arrow key.

This lesson has introduced you to working with fonts and changing the style and size of your text. In the next lesson, you'll learn to further enhance your document by adding headers and footers.

Adding Headers and Footers

In this lesson, you'll learn to enhance your document by adding headers and footers.

Headers and footers add information to your document that you want to include on every page or on selected pages. WordPerfect gives you the option of including headers and footers on every page, even numbered pages, or odd numbered pages. You can create headers and footers that are up to an entire page in length; however, for most purposes you'll use only one or two lines.

Adding Headers

The procedure for adding headers is a simple one:

1. Place the cursor at the top of the first page on which you want to include the header.

2. Open the Layout menu or press Shift-F8 (Format).

3. Choose **Page** or type **2**.

4. When the Format: Page menu is displayed, type **3** to select Headers.

5. Type 1 to select Header A.

6. Select which pages you want to add the header to (type 2 for Every Page, 3 for Odd pages, or 4 for Even Pages). The header screen is then displayed (see Figure 17-1).

7. Enter the text on the header screen as you would any text in the document. (You can choose different text styles, if you wish.)

8. When you've finished entering text, press F7 (Exit) or click the right mouse button twice.

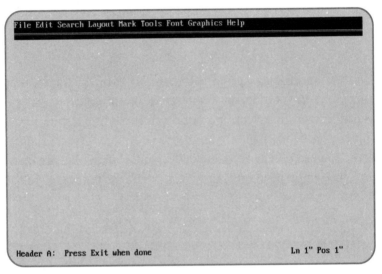

Figure 17-1. The header screen.

WordPerfect then adds the header you specified to the top of every page. You can cancel or modify the header at any time (these procedures are explained later in this lesson). If you want to display the header code WordPerfect placed in your document, press Alt-F3 to reveal codes (see Figure 17-2).

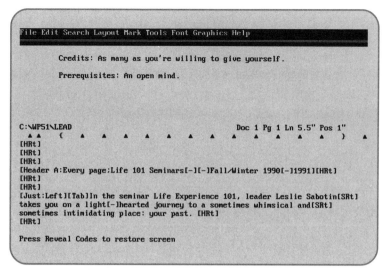

Figure 17-2. Looking at the header code.

Adding Footers

To add a footer follow these steps:

1. Place the cursor at the top of the first page on which you want to include the footer.

2. Open the Layout menu or press Shift-F8 (Format).

3. Choose Page or type 2.

4. When the Format: Page menu is displayed, type 4 to select Footers.

5. Type 1 to select Footer A.

6. Select which pages you want to add the footer to (type 2 for Every Page, 3 for Odd pages, or 4 for Even Pages). The footer screen is then displayed.

7. Enter the text on the footer screen as you would any text in the document.

8. When you've finished entering text, press F7 (Exit) or double-click the right mouse button.

The footer is then added to your document and will appear on every printed page, unless you discontinue the footer at some point later in the document.

Editing Headers and Footers

WordPerfect enables you to make changes to headers and footers easily. To edit a header, follow these steps:

1. Reveal codes by pressing Alt-F3.

2. Place the cursor on the code for the header or footer you want to modify.

3. Open the Layout menu or press Shift-F8 (Format).

4. Choose Page or type 2.

5. When the Format: Page menu is displayed, type 3 to select Headers or 4 to select Footers.

6. Select Header A or B or Footer A or B, depending on which item you want to edit.

7. Type 5 to select Edit.

8. Edit the text on the header or footer screen as you would any text in the document.

9. When you've finished entering text, press F7 (Exit) or double-click the right mouse button.

Canceling Headers and Footers

You can start and stop headers and footers at any point in your document. To quit headers and footers, follow these steps:

1. Move the cursor to the top of the first page on which you want the header or footer continued.

2. Open the Layout menu or press Shift-F8 (Format).

3. Choose **Page** or type **2**.

4. When the Format: Page menu is displayed, type **3** to select Headers or **4** to select Footers.

5. Select Header A or B or Footer A or B, depending on which item you want to cancel.

6. Type **1** to select Discontinue.

7. Press F7 (Exit) or double-click the right mouse button.

WordPerfect then discontinues the header and/or footer beginning with the page you specified. If you want to restart the header or footer on another page later in the document, you can simply repeat the procedure for creating headers and footers.

This lesson introduced you to the procedures for adding headers and footers to your document. The next lesson shows you how to add page breaks and page numbers.

Adding Page Breaks and Page Numbers

In this lesson, you'll learn to add page breaks and page numbers to your document.

Adding Page Breaks

WordPerfect automatically takes care of page breaks for you. (A *page break* is a line on-screen showing where WordPerfect begins printing the next page.) If you wish, however, you can manually insert page breaks.

When you set up the paper size and margins for your document, WordPerfect automatically determines how many lines of text will fit on a printed page. (The placement of the page break also depends on the size of the font you are using for your text.)

Automatic Page Breaks

For documents longer that one page, WordPerfect automatically inserts a page break code in the text and shows the page break on–screen as a dashed line (see Figure 18-1). This is known as a *soft page break*. In the Reveal Codes screen, the automatic page break is shown as [SPg].

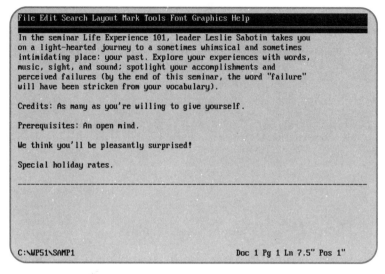

Figure 18-1. An automatic page break.

When you edit the text in the document, WordPerfect takes care of moving the text and rebreaking the page for you.

Manual Page Breaks

There may be times when you want to be sure that certain items print on certain pages. In this instance, you'll want to insert a manual page break. To manually break pages, follow these steps:

1. Place the cursor on the line where you want to break the page.

2. Press Ctrl-Enter.

WordPerfect inserts a double-dashed line at that point in the document (see Figure 18-2). This is known as a hard page break. In the Reveal Codes screen, the code appears as [HPg].

```
File Edit Search Layout Mark Tools Font Graphics Help

    Class                Date   Instructor        Cost

    Life Experiences    01/23/91   Sabotin         75.00
    Parenting           01/30/91   Murray          50.00
    Writing Seminar     02/23/91   Marshall        35.00
    Visualization       02/28/91   Sabotin         50.00
    Dreaming Awake      03/15/91   Reed            60.00

==============================================================================



C:\WP51\SAMP1                              Doc 1 Pg 2 Ln 1" Pos 1"
```

Figure 18-2. A manual page break.

If you want to remove the manual page break, simply display the Reveal Codes screen (by pressing Alt-F3), and delete the code.

Adding Page Numbers

When you want to add page numbers to the headers or footers in your document, follow these steps:

1. Place the cursor on the page where you want to begin numbering.

2. Open the Layout menu or press Shift-F8 (Format).

3. Choose Page or type 2.

4. Type 6 to select Page Numbering.

5. Type 4 to select Page Number Position.

6. Type the number that represents the page number position you want to use.

7. Press F7 (Exit) twice.

WordPerfect then inserts the code [Pg Numbering:] to mark the place for the page number and will begin numbering pages automatically.

You can also add page numbers to your document without placing them in a header or footer. To do so, follow these steps:

1. Place the cursor on the page where you want to begin numbering.

2. Open the Layout menu or press Shift-F8 (Format).

3. Choose Page or type 2.

4. Type 6 to select Page Numbering.

5. Type 4 to select Page Number Position.

6. Type the number that represents the page number position you want to use.

7. Press F7 (Exit) twice.

This lesson introduced you to adding page breaks and page numbers in your document. The next lesson shows you how to work with WordPerfect's spelling checker.

Lesson 19

Using the Spelling Checker

In this lesson, you will learn to work with WordPerfect's spelling checker.

Working with the Spelling Checker

WordPerfect's spelling checker can locate the following problems in your text:

- Misspelled words

- Double words

- Incorrect capitalization

As talented as the spelling checker is, it won't catch the following errors:

- Incorrect words that are spelled correctly (such as *coke* for *code*).

- Words used in the wrong context (such as *you're* for *your*).

- Typos that are stand-alone letters surrounded with spaces (such as *y* or *t*).

With WordPerfect, you have the option of checking the spelling of entire documents or individual words, text blocks, or pages.

Starting the Spelling Checker

Before you start the spelling checker, first move the cursor to the text you want to check.

Entire document	Place the cursor anywhere in the document
Individual word	Place the cursor on the word
Text block	Move the cursor to the block, press Alt-F4, and select the block
Single page	Place the cursor at the top of the page

After you have selected the text, follow these steps to start the spelling checker.

1. Press Ctrl-F2 (Spell) or open the Tools menu and choose **Spell**.

2. Type the number for the type of text to be checked (Figure 19-1 shows the options):

   1 to check an individual word

   2 to check a single page

   3 to check an entire document

If you are checking a block of text, you can skip this step.

WordPerfect then checks the text you selected. When it finds a word it doesn't recognize, it highlights the word and displays a list of alternative spellings (see Figure 19-2). You can choose one of the displayed spellings by typing the letter in front of the word you want or you can select one of these options:

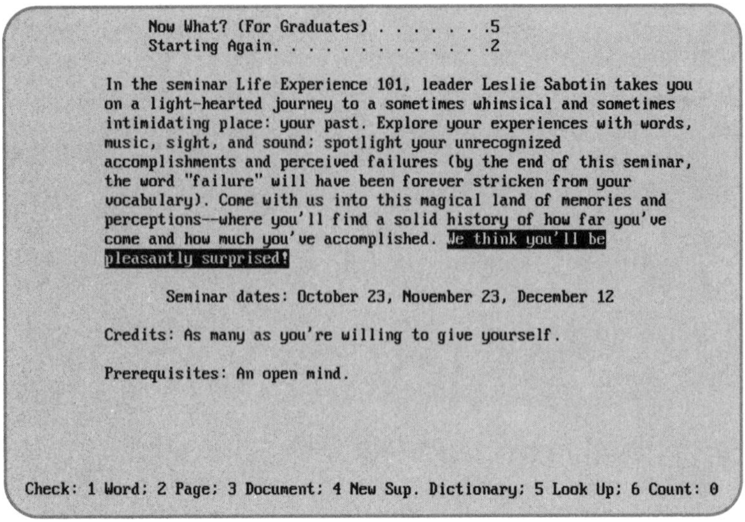

```
        Now What? (For Graduates) . . . . . .5
        Starting Again. . . . . . . . . . . .2

    In the seminar Life Experience 101, leader Leslie Sabotin takes you
    on a light-hearted journey to a sometimes whimsical and sometimes
    intimidating place: your past. Explore your experiences with words,
    music, sight, and sound; spotlight your unrecognized
    accomplishments and perceived failures (by the end of this seminar,
    the word "failure" will have been forever stricken from your
    vocabulary). Come with us into this magical land of memories and
    perceptions--where you'll find a solid history of how far you've
    come and how much you've accomplished. We think you'll be
    pleasantly surprised!

        Seminar dates: October 23, November 23, December 12

    Credits: As many as you're willing to give yourself.

    Prerequisites: An open mind.



Check: 1 Word; 2 Page; 3 Document; 4 New Sup. Dictionary; 5 Look Up; 6 Count: 0
```

Figure 19-1. The spelling checker screen.

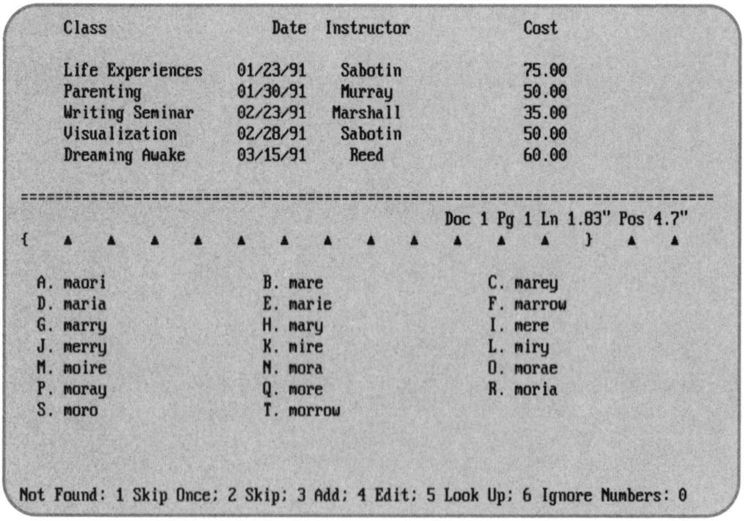

```
    Class                Date  Instructor        Cost

    Life Experiences    01/23/91  Sabotin        75.00
    Parenting           01/30/91  Murray         50.00
    Writing Seminar     02/23/91  Marshall       35.00
    Visualization       02/28/91  Sabotin        50.00
    Dreaming Awake      03/15/91  Reed           60.00

===============================================================================
                                    Doc 1 Pg 1 Ln 1.83" Pos 4.7"
{   ▲   ▲   ▲   ▲   ▲   ▲   ▲   ▲   ▲   ▲   ▲   ▲   }   ▲   ▲

A. maori            B. mare             C. marey
D. maria            E. marie            F. marrow
G. marry            H. mary             I. mere
J. merry            K. mire             L. miry
M. moire            N. mora             O. morae
P. moray            Q. more             R. moria
S. moro             T. morrow

Not Found: 1 Skip Once; 2 Skip; 3 Add; 4 Edit; 5 Look Up; 6 Ignore Numbers: 0
```

Figure 19-2. Displaying alternative spellings.

Skip Once	Allows you to skip over this occurrence of the word
Skip	Skips all occurrences of the word in the current document
Add	Enables you to add the word to WordPerfect's dictionary
Edit	Lets you type a correct spelling for the word
Look Up	Enables you to look up a different word
Ignore Numbers	Lets you bypass unusual numbers that WordPerfect automatically highlights

Looking Up Words You can have WordPerfect look up the spelling of a word for you. Simply press Ctrl-F2 (Spell), press **5**, and type the word. WordPerfect will check the word for you, and you can return to the document uninterrupted.

Word Count You can get a word count without going through a spell check. Simply press Ctrl-F2 (Spell) and type **6** to select Count. Without actually performing a spell check on your document, WordPerfect tallies the number of words and displays the result.

Creating Additional Dictionaries

When WordPerfect encounters a word it doesn't know, the program will highlight the word as though it is spelled incorrectly. You can create additional dictionaries to include words you use frequently, particularly if your work involves legal, medical, or technical terms that would be too specialized to appear in a traditional dictionary.

Each time you add a word to the WordPerfect dictionary (by selecting **Add** when the program highlights a misspelled word), WordPerfect adds the word to a file called WP{WP}US.SUP. This file serves as your own personal dictionary, containing all the words you add to the spelling checker.

You can create another personal dictionary file by following these steps:

1. Press Ctrl-F2 (Spell) or open the Tools menu and choose **Spell**.

2. Type **4** to select New Sup. Dictionary.

3. Type a name for the dictionary you want to create.

4. Press Enter.

Now that the new file is created, you can proceed with the spell check, adding words as necessary to the new dictionary file.

Leaving the Spelling Checker

The procedure for exiting the spelling checker is a simple one. When you're done checking your spelling, simply press F7 (Exit) to return to the document. If you want to stop the spelling checker before it's finished, press F1 (Cancel).

In this lesson, you've experimented with the spelling checker. The next lesson introduces you to the thesaurus.

Lesson 20

Using the Thesaurus

In this lesson, you'll work with WordPerfect's thesaurus.

Working with the Thesaurus

WordPerfect's thesaurus can help you find synonyms and antonyms for words in your document. To work with the thesaurus, follow these steps:

1. Open the document you want to work with.

2. Position the cursor on the word for which you want to find alternatives.

3. Open the Tools menu and choose Thesaurus, or press Alt-F1 (Thesaurus).

WordPerfect looks through its files to find possible alternatives to the word you've highlighted. The program then displays a list of words that you could use in place of the selected word (see Figure 20-1). At the bottom of the screen, you'll see a line of four options: Replace Word, View Doc, Look Up Word, and Clear Column.

109

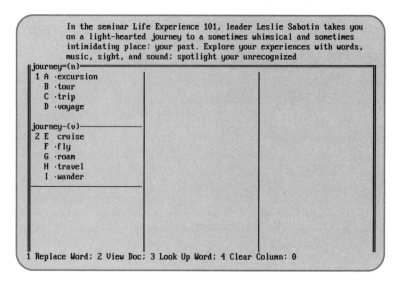

Figure 20-1. The Thesaurus screen.

Replacing Words

To select one of the displayed words as a replacement for the highlighted word, follow these steps:

1. Type 1 to select Replace Word.

2. After the prompt `Press letter for word`, type the letter that corresponds to the word you want to use.

WordPerfect replaces the highlighted word in the document with the word you specified.

Viewing the Document

You may want to go back to the document and review the context of the word you are thinking about replacing. WordPerfect makes this easy for you:

1. When the Thesaurus menu is displayed at the bottom of the screen, type 2 to select View Doc.

2. When you are finished reviewing the document, press F7 (Exit) to return to the Thesaurus screen.

Looking Up a Word

While you're using the Thesaurus, you may think of another word you'd like to find out about. You can look up another word from within the Thesaurus by following these steps:

1. Display the Thesaurus menu by pressing Alt-F1.

2. Type 3 to select Look Up Word.

3. Type the word you want to look up.

4. Press Enter.

WordPerfect searches the Thesaurus and displays alternative words for the word you specified.

Clearing Thesaurus Columns

As you work with the Thesaurus, the program places in columns the words you look up and the alternative words displayed by the Thesaurus. You can use the last option on the Thesaurus menu, Clear Column, to display columns of words that have been "bumped off" the screen by subsequent columns.

To clear columns, follow these steps:

1. Display the Thesaurus menu by pressing Alt-F1.

2. Type 4 to select Clear Column.

WordPerfect then displays columns you filled earlier in the current worksession.

Exiting the Thesaurus

Again, the trusty F7 (Exit) key comes in handy when you're ready to return to the document. If you press F7 (Exit) before you have selected any of the options on the Thesaurus menu, WordPerfect returns you to the document with the highlighted word unchanged. If you used any of the options or replaced a word, you will find the word replaced when you press F7 to return to the document.

In this lesson, you explored the process of using the thesaurus to help strengthen and add variety to your word choice. In the next lesson, you'll learn how to work with two documents at once in a WordPerfect worksession.

Lesson 21

Working with Two Documents

In this lesson, you'll learn to work with two WordPerfect documents on-screen at one time.

Working with Document Windows

In earlier lessons, you learned to reveal the hidden codes in your WordPerfect document by pressing Alt-F3. WordPerfect splits the screen into windows in order to show you the codes in the bottom half of the screen.

When you work with two documents, the basics are the same—except that in place of the Reveal Codes screen, you see another document.

Opening a Window

To open a second document window, follow these steps:

1. Display the first document you want to work with.

2. Open the Edit menu or press Ctrl-F3 (Screen).

3. Select **Window** or type **1**.

4. Type the number of lines you want the top window to include (for our example we entered 12).

5. Press Enter.

The screen is then split, showing a tab line separating the windows (see Figure 21-1). The arrows in the tab line point to the active window.

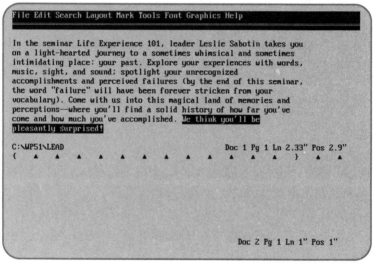

In the seminar Life Experience 101, leader Leslie Sabotin takes you on a light-hearted journey to a sometimes whimsical and sometimes intimidating place: your past. Explore your experiences with words, music, sight, and sound; spotlight your unrecognized accomplishments and perceived failures (by the end of this seminar, the word "failure" will have been forever stricken from your vocabulary). Come with us into this magical land of memories and perceptions—where you'll find a solid history of how far you've come and how much you've accomplished. We think you'll be pleasantly surprised!

Figure 21-1. An example of using two windows.

Moving between Windows

To move the cursor into the bottom window on the screen,

1. Open the Edit menu and choose Switch.

Or

2. Press Shift-F3 (Switch).

WordPerfect places the cursor in the bottom document, making that the active window.

Retrieving Documents into a Window

To open an existing document and place it in the bottom window of your screen, follow these steps:

1. Position the cursor in the window into which you want to retrieve the file.

2. Open the File menu and choose **Retrieve** or press Shift-F10.

3. Type the path and name of the file you want to retrieve; then press Enter to continue.

WordPerfect then places the file in the active window.

Retrieving Documents You can also retrieve a file by using F5 (List Files). Press F5, press Enter, highlight the file you want, and press **1**.

Copying between Windows

To copy or move text from window to window, follow these steps:

1. Display the windows on the screen.

2. Position the cursor in the window from which you want to copy the text.

3. Highlight the text you want to copy.

4. Open the Edit menu and choose **Copy**.

5. Press Shift-F3 (Switch) to move to the second document.

6. Place the cursor where you want the copy to be inserted and press Enter.

WordPerfect then places the copy of the text in the second document.

Note: Remember to save your changes before you exit the document or close a window. Each file must be saved independently. To save the document, move to the window (by pressing Shift-F3, if necessary), and save the document as usual.

Closing Windows

When you want to close a window, follow these steps:

1. Move to the window you want to leave open.

2. Open the Edit menu or press Ctrl-F3 (Screen).

3. Choose **Window** or type **1**.

4. When you are asked to enter the number of lines, type **24**.

5. Press Enter.

The display of the other window is then suppressed.

When you want to close the document, do so by placing the cursor in the document you want to close and pressing F7 (Exit). If you haven't saved the file, you will be asked whether you want to do so.

Switching between Displays

Rather than displaying two documents in windows on the screen at one time, you can display two different full-page views of the documents and switch between them.

To display another full-page document, follow these steps:

1. When the first document is displayed on the screen, press Shift-F3 (Switch) or open the Edit menu and choose Switch.

2. Load or create the document as usual.

3. When you want to switch back to the first document display, press Shift-F3 (Switch) again.

In this lesson, you've learned about working with two documents at once. The next lesson teaches you how to work with your WordPerfect files.

Lesson 22

Managing Files

In this lesson, you'll learn to use the List Files screen to work with your WordPerfect files.

Displaying the List Files Screen

You use the List Files screen, shown in Figure 22-1, to perform a number of file-management procedures, including:

- Retrieving files
- Deleting files
- Moving files
- Renaming files
- Printing files
- Viewing files
- Changing directories
- Copying files
- Finding text strings within files
- Searching for files

```
11-12-80  04:21p              Directory C:\WP51\*.*
Document size:        0   Free: 8,177,664 Used:  3,327,509      Files:    104

   .  Current     <Dir>          ..    Parent     <Dir>
8514A    .URS    4,862  01-19-90 12:00p  ALTRNAT .WPK     919  01-19-90 12:00p
ARROW-22.WPG       187  01-19-90 12:00p  ATI     .URS   6,036  01-19-90 12:00p
BALLOONS.WPG     3,187  01-19-90 12:00p  BANNER-3.WPG     719  01-19-90 12:00p
BICYCLE .WPG       607  01-19-90 12:00p  BKGRND-1.WPG  11,391  01-19-90 12:00p
BORDER-8.WPG       215  01-19-90 12:00p  BULB    .WPG   2,101  01-19-90 12:00p
BURST-1 .WPG       819  01-19-90 12:00p  BUTTRFLY.WPG   5,349  01-19-90 12:00p
CALENDAR.WPG       371  01-19-90 12:00p  CERTIF  .WPG     679  01-19-90 12:00p
CHARACTR.DOC    43,029  01-19-90 12:00p  CHKBOX-1.WPG     653  01-19-90 12:00p
CLOCK   .WPG     1,811  01-19-90 12:00p  CNTRCT-2.WPG   2,753  01-19-90 12:00p
CODES   .WPM     7,403  01-19-90 12:00p  CONVERT .EXE 109,049  01-19-90 12:00p
CURSOR  .COM     1,452  01-19-90 12:00p  DEVICE-2.WPG     657  01-19-90 12:00p
DIPLOMA .WPG     2,413  01-19-90 12:00p  EGA512  .FRS   3,584  01-19-90 12:00p
EGAITAL .FRS     3,584  01-19-90 12:00p  EGASMC  .FRS   3,584  01-19-90 12:00p
EGAUND  .FRS     3,584  01-19-90 12:00p  EHANDLER.PS    2,797  11-06-89 12:00p
ENDFOOT .WPM     3,871  01-19-90 12:00p  ENHANCED.WPK   3,571  01-19-90 12:00p
EQUATION.WPK     2,974  01-19-90 12:00p  FIXBIOS .COM      50  01-19-90 12:00p
FLOPPY-2.WPG       475  01-19-90 12:00p  FLYER   .WP5   1,444  11-09-80 08:54p
FOOTEND .WPM     3,833  01-19-90 12:00p ▼ GAVEL   .WPG     887  01-19-90 12:00p

1 Retrieve; 2 Delete; 3 Move/Rename; 4 Print; 5 Short/Long Display;
6 Look; 7 Other Directory; 8 Copy; 9 Find; N Name Search: 6
```

Figure 22-1. The List Files screen.

To get to the List Files screen,

1. Open the File menu and choose **List Files,** or press F5 (List Files).

2. Type the drive and directory whose files you want to list.

3. Press Enter.

WordPerfect displays the List Files screen. You can then select one of the file management procedures described in the following sections. Two of these procedures (retrieving files and viewing files) have already been described in Lessons 8 and 9, so we have not repeated them here.

Deleting Files

The next option on the List Files menu is the Delete option. To delete files from the List Files screen,

1. Highlight the name of the file you want to delete.

2. Type 2 to select Delete.

3. When WordPerfect asks you to confirm that you want to delete the file, type Y.

Deleting Multiple Files You can delete multiple files by first marking a set of files with asterisks: To mark multiple files, simply highlight the file you want and type an asterisk(*). To select more than one file, repeat the steps for each file you want to mark. You can then delete the set of files by typing 2 to select Delete.

Moving Files

When you want to move a file from one directory to another, follow these steps:

1. Highlight the file you want to move.

2. Type 3 to select Move/Rename.

3. Type the path to the drive and directory where you want to move the file and press Enter.

Moving Multiple Files You can move multiple files by first marking a set of files with asterisks (as shown in the preceding tip). You can select all files in the current directory by pressing Alt-F5 or Home, *.

Renaming Files

Occasionally, you'll want to change the names of files you've created. To rename files, follow these steps:

1. Highlight the file you want to rename.

2. Type 3 to select Move/Rename.

3. Type the new name for the file.

4. Press Enter.

WordPerfect then renames the file as indicated.

Printing Files

In an earlier lesson, you learned to print your documents. However, in some cases, you may want to print a document without retrieving it. You can also use this feature to print several documents in a row. From the List Files screen:

1. Highlight the file you want to print.

2. Type 4 to select Print.

3. Answer the prompts to begin printing.

If you want to print more than one file, select the appropriate files on the List Files screen by highlighting the files you want and pressing *.

Controlling File Display

You have the option of changing how much information is displayed about each file on the List Files screen. To change the way files are displayed in the List Files screen, follow these steps:

1. Type 5 to select Short/Long Display.

2. Type 1 to select Short Display.

3. Press Enter (or, if you want to change the directory, type the path and press Enter).

121

WordPerfect then displays the files in the new short display. To return to the original display, simply repeat the preceding steps and type **2** to select Long Display.

Changing File Directories

As you know, WordPerfect enables you to set a default directory that the program automatically searches when you are loading or saving files. To change the drive and directory temporarily, follow these steps from the List Files screen:

1. Press 7 to select Other Directory.

2. Type the new drive and path.

3. Press Enter twice.

Changing the Drive and Directory Here's a shortcut for changing the default drive and directory for your WordPerfect files: Press F5 (List Files); type =; type the new drive and directory; press Enter; and press Esc.

Copying Files

To make a copy of a file from the List Files screen, follow these steps:

1. Highlight the file you want to copy.

2. Type 8 to select Copy.

3. Type the drive and path to which you want to copy the file. If you're copying to the same directory, enter a new name for the file.

4. Press Enter.

The file is then copied to the drive and directory you specified.

Copying Multiple Files You can copy multiple files by first marking a set of files with asterisks: To mark multiple files, simply highlight the file you want and press *. For each additional file, repeat this step. You can then copy the set of files by typing **8** to select Copy and specifying the directory you want the marked files copied to.

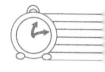

Finding Files

If you don't know the name of a file but you know a certain word or phrase used in the document, you can locate the file by searching for the word or phrase. To search for specific text in all files in a directory, follow these steps:

1. Press **9** to select Find.

2. Type **4** to select Entire Document.

3. Type the word (or phrase) you want to search for.

4. Press Enter.

WordPerfect then searches all the files in the directory for that text you entered. When the search is complete, WordPerfect displays a screen showing all the files with the text you specified. You can then look for the file you want and retrieve it as usual.

Searching for Files by Name

You can have WordPerfect locate a file when you know the name of the file (or something close). To search for a specific file, follow these steps:

1. Type **N** to select Name Search.

2. Begin typing the name of the file (if you only know a few letters—or even the first letter—that's okay; WordPerfect moves the highlight as soon as you begin typing).

WordPerfect automatically moves the cursor to the files that match the text you enter. Once the file is located, you can retrieve it as usual.

Summary

In this lesson, you've learned about working with the various options on the List Files screen. Now that you know how to create, edit, enhance, and print WordPerfect documents and you've mastered working with the WordPerfect files you create, you have completed your *10 Minute Guide to WordPerfect 5.1*.

At the back of this book there is a table of features, a Reveal Codes table, and the DOS Primer, organized so that you can easily find features and procedures not fully covered here.

If you want to further your experience with WordPerfect 5.1, you may want to consult the following books:

- *The First Book of WordPerfect 5.1*, by Kate Barnes

- *The Best Book of WordPerfect 5.1*, by Vincent Alfieri, revised by Ralph Blodgett

- *WordPerfect 5.1: Step-by-Step*, by Judd Robbins

- *WordPerfect 5.1 Bible*, by Susan Baake-Kelly

WordPerfect 5.1 Table of Features

Feature	Description	Menu Options	Keystrokes
Block	Selects text block	Edit, Block	Alt-F4
Cancel	Cancels operation		F1
Center	Centers text	Layout, Align, Center	Shift-F6
Copy	Copies block	Edit, Copy	Ctrl-F4, 1, 2
Delete	Deletes block	Edit, Delete	Del or Backspace
Document Compare	Allows you to compare two documents	Mark, Document Compare	Alt-F5, 6, 2
Endnote	Adds endnote	Layout, Endnote	Ctrl-F7, 2
Font change	Changes font	Font, Base Font	Ctrl-F8, 4
Footers	Adds footer	Layout, Page, 4	Shift-F8, 2, 4
Footnote	Adds footnote	Layout, Footnote, Create	Ctrl-F7, 1, 1
Graphics	Adds graphics elements to your document	Graphics, then Figure, Table Box, Text Box, or User Box, Create	Alt-F9, then 1, 2, 3, or 4, and 1
Hard page break	Inserts manual page break		Ctrl-Enter

Feature	Description	Menu Options	Keystrokes
Headers	Adds header	Layout, Page, 3	Shift-F8, 2, 3
Indent	Indents text	Layout, Align, Indent	F4 or Shift-F4
Justification	Sets alignment of text	Layout, Line, Justification	Shift-F8, 1, 3
Line draw	Lets you draw lines in your document	Tools, Line Draw	Ctrl-F3, 2
Line	Sets line spacing	Layout, Line, Line Spacing	Shift-F8, 1, 6
Macro	Defines a macro	Tools, Macro, Define	Ctrl-F10
Macro	Runs a macro	Tools, Macro, Execute	Alt-F9
Margins	Sets margins	Layout, Line	Shift-F8, 1, 7
Columns/table	Sets up columns and tables	Layout Columns or Tables	Alt-F7, 1 or 2
Move	Moves block	Edit, Move	Ctrl-F4, 1, 1
Outline	Sets up outline	Tools, Outline	Shift-F5, 4
Page numbers	Sets page numbers	Layout, Page, Page numbering	Shift-F8, 2, 6
Paper size	Sets paper size	Layout, Page, Paper Size/Type	Shift-F8, 2, 7
Password	Passwords file	File, Password, Add/Change	Ctrl-F5, 2
Printing	Sets printing options	File, Print	Shift-F7

Feature	Description	Menu Options	Keystrokes
Replace	Replaces text	Search, Replace	Alt-F2
Retrieve	Retrieves files	File, Retrieve	Shift-F10
Reveal Codes	Displays codes	Edit, Reveal Codes	Alt-F3
Save	Saves document or text block	File, Save	F10
Search	Searches for text	Search, Forward or Backward	F2 or Shift-F2
Setup	Controls basic system settings	File, Setup	Shift-F1
Spell	Spell checks document	Tools, Spell	Ctrl-F2
Summary	Displays file information	File, Summary	Shift-F8, 3, 5
Tabs	Controls tabs	Layout, Line, Tab Set	Shift-F8, 1, 8
Thesaurus	Runs thesaurus	Tools, Thesaurus	Alt-F1
Undelete	Cancels deletion	Edit, Undelete, Restore	F1, 1
Window	Displays second document window	Edit, Window	Ctrl-F3, 1

Reveal Codes

Here's a list of codes that relate to the lessons in this book. For a complete list of codes, see your WordPerfect manual or *The Best Book of WordPerfect 5.1.*

Code	Meaning	Code	Meaning
[Block]	Beginning of block	[Pg Num]	New page number
[BOLD][bold]	Bold ON off	[Pg Num Pos]	Page number position
[C/A/FlRt]	End of Tab Align or Flush Right	[REDLN][redln]	Redline font ON off
		[SHADW][shadw]	Shadow font ON off
[Center Pg]	Center page top to bottom	[SM CAP]	Small cap font ON
		[sm cap]	Small cap font off
[Cntr]	Center text	[SMALL][small]	Small font ON off
[Cndl EOP]	Conditional end of page	[SRt]	Soft return
		[STKOUT]	Strikeout font ON
[Col Def]	Column definition	[stkout]	Strikeout font off
[Col Off]	End of text columns	[SUBSCPT]	Subscript font ON
[Col On]	Start of text columns	[subscpt]	Subscript font off
[Comment]	Document comment	[SUPRSCPT]	Superscript font ON
[Date]	Date/Time function	[suprscpt]	Superscript font off
[DBL UND]	Double underline ON	[T/B Mar]	Top and bottom margin
[dbl und]	Double underline off	[Tab]	Tab
[DSRt]	Deletable soft return	[Tab Set]	Tab set
[Ext Large]	Extra large print	[UND][und]	Underline font ON off
[FINE][fine]	Fine font ON off	[VRY LARGE]	Very large font ON
[Flsh Rt]	Flush right text	[vry large]	Very large font off
[Font]	Base font		
[Footer]	Footer text		
[Header]	Header text		
[HRt]	Hard return		
[Hyph]	Hyphenation		
[HZone]	Hyphenation zone		
[Indent]	Indent		
[ITALC][italc]	Italic ON off		
[Just]	Justification		
[L/R Mar]	Left and right margins		
[LARGE][large]	Large font ON off		
[Mar Rel]	Margin release		
[Outln]	Outline		
[Ovrstk]	Overstrike		
[Paper Sz/Typ]	Paper size and type		

DOS Primer

This section highlights some of the DOS procedures you will use during your work with WordPerfect and other programs.

Preparing Disks

The first step in preparing disks to store programs and data is formatting the disks.

What Is Formatting? The formatting procedure writes important information to the disk, preparing it to store data. You cannot place any information—programs or data of any kind—on a new disk before the disk is formatted. Formatting also erases any information on a diskette. *Do not* format your hard disk drive, however, because formatting a hard disk erases all programs and information on the hard disk.

1. Turn the computer on.

2. If the system asks you for the date and time, type these in and press Enter after each entry. (Not all systems ask for the date and time.) Enter the date in the form MM:DD:YY (such as 11:23:90) and the time in the form HH:MM:SS (such as 08:30:00).

3. Change to the drive and directory that contains your DOS files. For example, if your DOS files are in C:\DOS, type **cd\ DOS** at the C> prompt and press Enter.

4. Insert the first blank disk in the A: or B: drive and close the drive door.

5. Type **FORMAT A:** or **FORMAT B:** and press Enter. The system will tell you to insert the disk (which you've already done).

6. Press Enter. The system then begins formatting the disk. When the format is complete, the system asks whether you want to format another.

7. Type **Y**. If you want to format additional disks, then repeat these steps.

Labeling Disks While the disk is being formatted, you may want to use the time to write the labels for the disks. Be sure to write on the labels before you attach them to the diskettes. (If you've already placed the labels on the diskettes, write on the labels using a felt-tip pen. The hard point of a ball-point pen can damage the surface of a diskette.)

You then repeat these steps as many times as necessary to format the backup disks for your WordPerfect program. Now you're ready to make the copy.

Making Backup Copies

To make a copy of your WordPerfect program, follow these steps:

1. Place the original WordPerfect disk in drive A.

2. Place the blank, formatted disk to which you want to copy in drive B.

3. Type **DISKCOPY A: B:** and press Enter. (If you have two drives that are different sizes—such as one 5.25 and one 3.5 inch drive—or you have only one floppy drive, use **DISKCOPY A: A:** instead.)

   The system then copies to drive B the information from the disk in drive A. When the operation is complete, the system asks whether you want to copy another disk.

4. Type **Y**.

DOS Confusion If you're having trouble under-standing some of these commands, don't worry—the formatting and copying procedures are part of DOS, your computer's operating system. For more information about using DOS, see the *The First Book of MS-DOS*.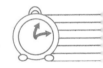

Repeat the DISKCOPY procedure until you've copied all your WordPerfect disks. Now you're ready to install the program (see inside front cover).

Working with Directories

DOS enables you to organize your files in directories and sub-directories. You can think of this organization as a tree structure—each directory can have subdirectories (like the branches splitting off the trunk of a tree).

Making Directories

To create a directory, you use the MD (Make Directory) command. Follow these steps:

131

1. At the DOS prompt, type **MD** *drive:\ directoryname*.

In this example, substitute the name for the directory you are creating in place of *directoryname*.

2. Press Enter.

This command causes DOS to create the directory under the name you specified and on the drive you specified.

 Root Directory The root directory is the main directory on your disk (the trunk of the tree). All other directories and subdirectories are divisions of the root directory.

Note: You do not need to create a directory in order to run WordPerfect; the installation program takes care of this for you. You may want to create additional directories to store your data files, however.

Moving to a Directory

You need to be able to move from directory to directory. To change directories, you use the CD (Change Directory) command:

1. At the DOS prompt, type **CD** \ *directoryname*

In this command line, the backslash (\) tells DOS to begin at the root directory and move to the directory you specified under the root. You use the backslash to separate all directories and subdirectories in a command line. For example, if you wanted to move to a subdirectory of the directory shown above, the command line would look like this:

```
CD \directoryname\subdirectoryname
```

2. Press Enter.

DOS then moves to the directory or subdirectory you specified.

Displaying Directory Contents

To see which files are stored in a directory, you use the command DIR (Directory):

1. Change to the directory you want to display.

2. Type **DIR**.

3. Press Enter.

DOS then displays a list of all the files in the current directory.

Working with Files

DOS also includes commands you can use to work with the files you create. This section briefly introduces the procedures for copying, deleting, and renaming files.

Copying Files

When you want to copy files using DOS, you use the COPY command:

1. Move to the directory that stores the file (or files) you want to copy.

2. Type the command line:

```
COPY filename1 filename2
```

In this command line, *filename1* is the name of the existing file you want to copy, and *filename2* is the new name you want the copy of the file to be given. If you want to copy the file to a different drive or directory, specify the path before *filename*.

133

3. Press Enter.

DOS then copies the file and places the copy in the current directory.

Deleting Files

When you delete files using DOS, you use the ERASE (or DEL) command:

1. Move to the directory that stores the file you want to erase.

2. Type the command line:

   ```
   ERASE filename
   ```
   Or

   ```
   DEL filename
   ```

3. Press Enter.

4. When DOS asks you for confirmation, type Y.

DOS then deletes the file.

Renaming Files

You use the RENAME (or REN) command to rename files in DOS:

1. Move to the directory that stores the file you want to rename.

2. Type the command line:

   ```
   RENAME filename1 filename2
   ```
   Or

   ```
   REN filename1 filename2
   ```

In this command line, *filename1* is the name of the existing file, and *filename2* is the new name you want to assign to the file.

3. Press Enter.

DOS then renames the file and keeps it in the current directory.

For more information about using DOS commands, see *The First Book of MS-DOS*.

Index

individual characters with Backspace, 24
individual characters with Del, 25
text blocks, 59-60
dictionaries
creating additional, 107-108
directories
changing, 122
creating, 131
displaying contents of, 43, 133
moving to, 132
disks
preparing, 129-134
displaying
codes, 34-35
directory contents, 43, 133
files, 121-122
header codes, 97
menus, 8-10
switching between windows, 116-117
tab line, 76-77
documents
checking word context, 110
editing, 23-28
naming, 39-40
previewing, 46-47
retrieving, 42-45
saving, 38-41
spell checking, 105-108
starting, 12-15
using document windows, 113-117
viewing, 44-45
word count, 107
working with tabs, 75-81
DOS primer
copying program disks, 130
creating directories, 131
deleting files, 134
moving to directories, 132

preparing disks, 129-134
renaming files, 134-135
dot leaders, 80-81
double-clicking, 16
dragging, 16

E

editing
codes, 36
documents, 23-28
footers, 98
headers, 98
entering text, 12-13

F

files
changing directories, 122
controlling display of, 121-122
copying, 122
deleting, 119-120, 134
displaying directory contents, 133
finding, 123
managing, 118-124
moving, 120
naming, 39-40
printing, 121
renaming, 120, 134
retrieving, 42-45
saving, 38-41
searching for, 123
starting document, 12-15
viewing, 44-45
finding files, 123
fonts
changing, 91-94
defined, 89
finding out what your printer supports, 89-90

manual page breaks, 101-102
margins, 70-71
   left and right, 73-74
   top and bottom, 72-74
   working with, 71-74
menus
   opening, 19-21
   pull-down, 17
   selecting with keyboard, 17-21
   setting up, 8-10
   using, 16-21
   using speed keys, 18
mini-saves, 40-41
modes
   insert, 27
   preview, 46-47
   typeover, 27-28
mouse
   basic mouse operations, 16-17
moving the cursor, 13
   setting up, 7-10
moving
   between document windows,
     114
   files, 120
   tabs, 79-80
   text, 58-59
   to a directory, 132

N—O

naming
   documents, 39-40
numbering pages, 102-103
opening
   menus, 19-21
   windows, 113-114
options
   choosing, 20-21
   selecting, 16-18

P

page breaks
   adding, 100-103
   automatic, 100-101
   manual, 101-102
page numbers
   adding, 102-103
paper
   choosing size and type, 70-71
paths, 38
pointing, 16
preparing disks, 129-134
preview mode, 46-47
previewing
   documents, 46-47
Print menu
   options on the, 50-51
   using the, 49
printer
   determining font capability of,
     89-90
printing
   checking printer setup, 47-48
   files, 121
   initializing printer, 48-49
preparing, 47-51
   text blocks, 62
   using the Print menu, 49-51
pull-down menus, 17

Q—R

quitting
   WordPerfect, 10-11
renaming
   files, 120, 134-135
replacing
   globally, 69
   selectively, 67-69
   text, 67-69